"A writer is someone who pays
to listen to what others aren[...]
silence in the midst of all the n[...]
   In the silent courtrooms, s[...]
   whom no one else can,
   Being the voice in a language where all there could
   comprehend,
   Words which have been the last ... or one whom he'll
   see again,
   Each door shut as verdicts bring them to an end.
   But the story lives through his pen ... as he recalls
   each one, fifty years later...
A man who has loved to write all his life, recalls each experience since he was nineteen years old; his very first job till now. With much delight, pleasure, honour and clarity he shares with us this book beyond the courtrooms. As a dedication to his fifty years in serving the various courts since 1 September 1967, Mr Siva puts all he has in this very first book of his. May it speak to each one just the way he has written it."

Nisa Raja Sekaran,
Senior Executive (CJTD); Assistant Registrar, State Courts

"This page-turner is a fascinating read that offers the reader an inside look into some of the most noteworthy cases to be heard at the High Courts. Mr Siva has mined his extensive experience as a seasoned court interpreter and offered valuable insights into human nature and Singapore society. This is a must-read for all who share an interest in the workings of our justice system as well as the crimes that have shocked Singapore."

Vanita Kaneson,
Senior Court Counsellor, State Courts

"Mr Siva is extraordinary in many ways. He embraces the spirit of lifelong learning. His professional working life has spanned the Supreme Court, the State Courts and the Family Justice Courts in the Judiciary. I am fascinated and hasten to congratulate Mr Siva for having produced a masterful work. What has emerged is an interesting book that covers many court cases in great detail, based on his wealth of experience as a veteran court interpreter. It offers valuable insights into our society over several decades. I recommend it heartily to all who share an interest in the workings of our justice system."

Daniel Ang,
Deputy Director, Language Services, State Courts

"As a student interpreter my very first exposure to quality interpretation was watching Mr Siva interpret for a witness in a murder trial. That observation was etched in my mind and has since served as a yardstick for quality interpretation."

Mary Doris Gnanaraj,
Assistant Director, Language Services, State Courts

"I love this book! I know no one else who could have written a book like this. Mr Siva has the real-life experience, passion for his job and life. He has generously shared what he has learnt with all of us."

Jackie Chong,
Senior Language Executive, State Courts

"Mr Siva has been a colleague, a friend and a mentor to me. A man who is very experienced in the courts in Singapore. I am very privileged to have crossed paths with him."

Muhammad Rijal,
Senior Language Executive, State Courts

"For one who has been around for so many years, and yet still has the desire to contribute, that's very inspiring. Mr Siva is always ready to share and guide. All I need to do is approach him, and I'll have my queries answered."

Zaini Sojah,
Senior Language Executive, State Courts

"Heartiest congratulations and best wishes on your fifty years of achievement in the Language Services with the Judiciary. Through the years, you have been a great mentor, guide and friend to all of us. You have always been there to lend a helping hand, to teach and inspire junior officers like me. The knowledge, skills and experience that you have shared are bountiful. I am honoured to be among the few privileged officers to have had the opportunity to work with you in my twenty-five years in the State Courts. I have always admired the love that you have for the Tamil Language and the little poems that you write for us on special occasions. Thank you for always being there to guide and inspire us. Here's wishing you all the very best in the years to come."

Jayanthi Jaganathan,
Language Services, State Courts

*Happy Reading
Angelin*

BEYOND A REASONABLE DOUBT

BEYOND A REASONABLE DOUBT

GIVING VOICE TO THE ACCUSED

N SIVANANDAN

Marshall Cavendish Editions

© 2019 Marshall Cavendish International (Asia) Private Limited

Published by Marshall Cavendish Editions
An imprint of Marshall Cavendish International

A member of the
Times Publishing Group

All rights reserved

No part of this publication may be reproduced, stored in a retrieval system or transmitted, in any form or by any means, electronic, mechanical, photocopying, recording or otherwise, without the prior permission of the copyright owner. Requests for permission should be addressed to the Publisher, Marshall Cavendish International (Asia) Private Limited, 1 New Industrial Road, Singapore 536196. Tel: (65) 6213 9300.
E-mail: genref@sg.marshallcavendish.com
Website: www.marshallcavendish.com/genref

The publisher makes no representation or warranties with respect to the contents of this book, and specifically disclaims any implied warranties or merchantability or fitness for any particular purpose, and shall in no event be liable for any loss of profit or any other commercial damage, including but not limited to special, incidental, consequential, or other damages.

Other Marshall Cavendish Offices:
Marshall Cavendish Corporation, 99 White Plains Road, Tarrytown NY 10591-9001, USA • Marshall Cavendish International (Thailand) Co Ltd, 253 Asoke, 12th Flr, Sukhumvit 21 Road, Klongtoey Nua, Wattana, Bangkok 10110, Thailand • Marshall Cavendish (Malaysia) Sdn Bhd, Times Subang, Lot 46, Subang Hi-Tech Industrial Park, Batu Tiga, 40000 Shah Alam, Selangor Darul Ehsan, Malaysia.

Marshall Cavendish is a registered trademark of Times Publishing Limited

National Library Board, Singapore Cataloguing-in-Publication Data

Name(s): N. Sivanandan.
Title: Beyond a reasonable doubt : giving voice to the accused / N. Sivanandan.
Description: Singapore : Marshall Cavendish Editions, [2019]
Identifier(s): OCN 1090528691 | ISBN 978-981-4841-48-1 (paperback)
Subject(s): LCSH: Trials—Singapore—History. | Court interpreting and translating—Singapore. | N. Sivanandan.
Classification: DDC 345.07095957--dc23

Printed in Singapore

Cover photo by VikaSuh from Shutterstock.

For my parents,
who supported my dreams and
encouraged me throughout my career.

CONTENTS

Author's Note   13
Acknowledgements   15

PART 1

  The role of the interpreter   18
  My dream – but how did I become an interpreter?   27

The Cases:

  01 First appearance in court   36
     A gruesome gang rape

  02 My first murder trial   46
     A man kills his friend

  03 One of my earlier murder trials   54
     A drinking session turns ugly

  04 Delivering the death verdict   60
     A father's love ends in tragedy

  05 A charge of culpable homicide   65
     Spousal killing

  06 Another case of alcohol-related death   70
     Passion takes the better of them

  07 A difficult and challenging trial   76
     The result of uncontrollable anger

  08 "You interpret with so much confidence."   82
     The failed conspiracy

  09 A killing in my neighbourhood   90
     The case of a triangular love affair

10	Interpreting an unfamiliar accent *A careless woman pays*	95
11	A successful appeal *Everyone deserves a fair trial*	101
12	One of my longest trials *An unusual unlawful assembly*	107
13	An interesting case that I followed *Morbid jealousy*	115
14	A case that attracted international media *The riot that shook the nation*	125

My journey through the Judiciary — 134

Reflections — 163

PART 2

Opening of the legal year — 174

The jury trial — 175

Judicial Committee of the Privy Council — 177

Plea of Clemency — 179

References for the cases mentioned — 183

AUTHOR'S NOTE

Some time in September 2016, during a work discussion with Judge Bala Reddy in his chambers, he suggested that I write about my long experiences in the courts. The former principal district judge of the Community Justice Tribunals Division felt I should share with my younger colleagues what I had learnt in the Subordinate Courts, the State Courts and the High Court.

In all, I have completed more than five decades as an interpreter in the Judiciary, two decades of which were at the High Court. Judge Reddy had himself spent more than three decades both on the Bench and as a leading prosecuting officer of the Attorney-General's Chambers. Convinced that the interpreter is the extra element, the 'personal touch' as the 'voice box' of the witness, he was of the view that I should compile a variety of interesting cases that highlighted my role as an interpreter – especially the particular events during trials; the behaviour and mannerisms of counsel and deputies; the use of language by witnesses; the interpretation difficulties I had and how I overcame them.

I have often shared my courtroom knowledge and experiences with close colleagues and friends, and have thought about documenting my experiences. Motivated and encouraged by Judge Reddy, I spent several months in 2016 working on the book, recalling some of the more difficult trials that I had been involved in, their witnesses and the evidence as it unfolded in court. I then had to collect the cases from the law reports. My immediate colleagues Jackie, Rijal and Nisa came to my rescue; without their help, this assignment would have been almost impossible. Jackie spent many hours in the library on the seventh floor during her lunch breaks, and when she had time in between consultations. Her enthusiasm really spurred me on.

Together we collected the relevant material for the book. I did receive help from other colleagues too and friends in the legal fraternity, Rakesh Vasu and Amolat Singh to mention a few. Assistance from ex-judge Roy Neighbour was readily forthcoming.

I selected some fourteen cases dating back to a trial in 1969. Invariably, more of the cases came from the High Court where I had spent some twenty years and involved murder, rape and robbery.

This book gives an insight into the important role an interpreter has in the smooth functioning of the Judiciary, and I hope that it also shows the generation of today that the art of interpreting with accuracy is not only about the language but the emotion of the witness on the stand – a proficiency that is acquired over years of practice.

Whilst I acknowledge the help received from my ex-colleagues and friends, and am eternally grateful to them for making this book possible, the views expressed in this book are wholly my own, and they do not attempt to reflect the official position or views of the Judiciary (and its members) or the various departments which I have worked in at those various times. I have also sought to be accurate but if there are any remaining errors, they are entirely mine. I thank you for reading.

N Sivanandan
April 2019

ACKNOWLEDGEMENTS

I am most grateful to Judge Reddy for his encouragement and motivation without whose inspiration this book would never have materialised.

My thanks also go to:

- Kokilavani, Sathiya Krishnamoorthy (currently with Singapore Institute of Technology), Sumathi, Anita Sandra (Language Services), Rijal Muhammad
- Nisa Raja and Vanita Kaneson (both of CJTD) for diligently vetting the script at short notice
- Jackie Chong, for assisting in collecting case material and always being there for serious deliberations from as early as 7.30am on many days
- Those helping hands of the State Courts whose names may have been omitted for mention
- My wife Vimala who sacrificed hours of sleep working on this book with me

PART 1

THE ROLE OF THE INTERPRETER

Ask a serving interpreter in the courts how he or she finds the job and the answer invariably will be "interesting and challenging ... but not easy." Below are two scenarios that show why interpreting in courts is not as easy as it may appear to be.

Scenario 1

Lawyer: (Posing question to witness)...Where were you at 8.00pm on 14 May 2008? (Interpreter interprets to witness. The witness rattles away. Court awaits witness's answer... Losing his patience with the witness, the judge interjects...)

Judge: Witness, the question is simple. Please answer the question directly...Mr Interpreter...what has the witness been saying?

Interpreter: Your Honour, he says...that on 14 May 2008 he left his workplace at 2pm and proceeded to Tekka...there he met an old friend...they spoke for a while...then the friend told him to wait...and proceeded to run an errand..then...

Judge: Mr Interpreter please tell the witness to listen to the question carefully and answer the question to the point...and not to deviate from the issue.

The scenario shows the key role the interpreter plays in a bilingual courtroom, and the difficulties encountered when a witness becomes difficult or long-winded, or blatantly refuses to answer the question put to him. The interpreter not only has to translate what a witness says, but he has to coax the witness to answer to the point. And when a witness beats about the bush with his answers, the court may lose patience with the witness – and even with the interpreter!

Another scenario...
Lawyer: Witness, in your statement to the police, you said that on 21 July 2007 you arrived at the bus stop at Selegie Road at 5.10pm. However, in your statement in court this morning, you said on 21 July 2007 at about 5.10pm you were at a relative's place with a group of friends having a few drinks. Can you please explain the discrepancy? (Witness speaks in Tamil)

Interpreter: Your Honour, on the day and time in question, I was at my relative's place.

Judge: Does that mean you were not at the bus stop at the material time? If that is so, why did you say differently in your statement to the police? (Question interpreted to witness)

Interpreter: I did tell the police officer but he did not interpret what I had said.

Judge: Was the statement not read over to you and explained to you? Why did you not make the necessary amendment? (Interpreted to witness)

Interpreter: I did not understand the Tamil spoken by the recording officer.

Judge: Do you understand the court interpreter's Tamil?

Interpreter: The court interpreter's Tamil is slightly better than the Tamil spoken by the police officer.

In this scenario, the witness claims not to have understood a previous translation. Sometimes it takes much effort on the part of the interpreter to make a witness fully understood. An accused person may admit a charge, yet dispute the facts of the case as read out by the prosecuting officer.

I have come across people who think interpreting is just oral translation. "What is difficult about interpreting?" If a witness says "Go" in, for example, Tamil, the interpreter says "Go" in English.

One must encounter a difficult situation in the midst of a lengthy trial when the parties split hairs over simple words to realise the predicaments an interpreter faces. Interpretation/translation can be fairly difficult depending on the situation and the character of the testifying witness. Even strong and vulgar language must be interpreted. (See the case of 'The result of uncontrollable anger'.)

Difficulties may arise from the time a witness takes the stand or in the midst of his testimony when the witness tries to conceal some truth and in the process comes under severe scrutiny. Exercising his right to speak in any language he chooses, a witness can opt to change from one language to another at any stage of the trial.

It is the primary duty of the interpreter therefore to understand the entire proceedings of the trial, interpret to the witness accurately in the language he has chosen, receive his answer/explanation and put it across to the court clearly and precisely. This the interpreter is expected to do with the standard of professionalism expected of him, without any prejudice or bias, making sure that every bit of the evidence is adequately explained to the witness.

It is therefore extremely important for the interpreter to go over the facts patiently and convey to the accused person the full meaning of the statement, sometimes by asking additional questions to seek clarification. There have been instances where an accused person disputed some portions of the statement but after a lengthy explanation by an interpreter, his doubts are cleared, thanks to the skill of the experienced interpreter.

The interpreter, in the execution of his duty, must therefore be extremely alert throughout the trial and possess adequate knowledge in the languages he is proficient in. In a trial where the material witness speaks in the vernacular language, the role of the interpreter becomes even more crucial. The lawyers and trial judges, if they do not understand the language of the witness, would be entirely dependent on the interpreter.

When I failed to recall the right word

Sometimes, an interpreter can be stuck for words in the course of an interpretation – and cannot recall a commonly used, simple word. An interpreter can find himself lost; his memory can unbelievably fail. The consequence is pathetic, the embarrassment painful. The interpreter must console himself – he is not a mobile dictionary with an impeccable memory!

In the course of my many years interpreting, I have on a few occasions been in difficult and sometimes embarrassing situations.

I found myself in such a situation in a case heard in the old District and Magistrate's Courts.

If I remembered it rightly, it was a preliminary inquiry into a foiled robbery attempt which resulted in a victim's death.

The Deputy Public Prosecutor (DPP) was someone well-versed in the Tamil language. On the witness stand was a material witness in the trial, testifying in Tamil. In the midst of his lengthy questioning, the learned prosecutor posed questions about a chain, which was the subject of the charge. I interpreted the questions to the witness. In the course of interpreting I kept using the English word "chain". The Tamil term couldn't come to mind. I kept thinking hard for the Tamil equivalent for "chain". But no, I couldn't get it. The DPP went on with his questioning, still on the subject of the chain. I continued interpreting still very much unable to recall the Tamil equivalent for "chain". The DPP gave me a strange look, trying to gesticulate that I was using the English word. I soon realised the DPP's intention but failed to recall the Tamil term. The DPP then moved a little nearer to me and, when it was comfortable for him to do so, he whispered the Tamil word for "chain". Looking at the DPP with a great sense of gratitude, I took the cue from him and continued, now using the Tamil version of the word. Fortunately for me, the Magistrate on the Bench was Chinese. Little did the Magistrate realise how I had been struggling, unable to recall the appropriate word at the appropriate time.

The lengthy questioning of the material witness was finally over. The case was adjourned for further hearing to the next morning. What a relief it was for me. I was partly happy, partly upset. I looked at the DPP feeling extremely thankful for his timely gesture of assistance. Inside me, however, I felt real rotten and ashamed. How could I not have been able to recall such a simple, commonly used word! At the time of that incident I had spent more than five years in the service. "Thank you. I'm sorry," I told the learned prosecutor, shying myself away. He smiled and said, "It happens."

Even today, many years after the incident, I can't help feeling ashamed of myself for having forgotten such a simple word.

Can an interpreter's interpretation be challenged?
An interpreter is given sufficient training before his first appearance in court. To start with, an interpreter is expected to have the basic language qualifications. Candidates applying for an interpreter's job go through several interviews, both written and oral where they are 'grilled' by experienced language and trained administrative officers. The written language proficiency tests are set by Head Interpreters and a clear pass in these papers is required. The oral examinations test the candidates' ability to speak clearly and demonstrate their ability in basic oral interpretations. Passages are presented to candidates and they have to translate the given scripts sufficiently fast and well. These cover court material and current affairs to ensure the applicants possess knowledge in court matters. After all successful candidates will be interpreting in a courtroom environment.

Only after some weeks of basic training will a newly appointed interpreter be sent to open court to face witnesses in trials. These interpreters also need to attend classes during their trainee days. Therefore it is fair to say that the trainee undergoes sufficient thorough training before he faces his first "obstacle". To develop the trainee's confidence, he is placed under the watchful eye of a senior interpreter during the initial stages. Now the interpreter is all geared up to face a lawyer and witness in a trial.

Can an interpreter be faulted for a mistake in the course of interpreting? Mistakes can happen anywhere and in all sorts of situations. After all, to err is human. No mistake is deliberate. A mistake can arise if the witness and the interpreter misunderstand each other. Mistakes may also occur if the witness on the stand turns difficult or sometimes hostile. Under these circumstances much depends on how the scenario is handled by the judge hearing the case. Clear, neat clarification of any confused situation can prevent a misunderstanding by either party. So, to the question whether an interpreter can be faulted for 'misinterpretation', the answer probably will be "no". Deliberate misinterpretation is an impossibility. There are occasions when a witness is unclear in his testimony. This may lead to a misunderstanding and thus cause an error in interpretation. Parties before a judge are at liberty to clarify any issue that may result in confusion or misinterpretation!

An interpreter is a sworn officer of the court and will at all times live up to his oath of allegiance and interpret impartially to the best of his ability and knowledge. The fact that court interpreters have been relied on for many years is evident of the trust the public has in the interpreter's role. Their presence ensures the accused's right to defence and maintains the credibility of the judicial department. This is acknowledged by Singapore's founding father, the late Mr Lee Kuan Yew, who, in his address in Parliament, once upheld the integrity of interpreters, their importance and the special role they played in dispensing justice in the Republic.

Other duties that a court interpreter performs

Generally, the duty of a court interpreter is to assist witnesses in a trial, i.e. interpret to witnesses in languages/dialects they are most comfortable in. What else is an interpreter's job? How else does an interpreter assist the courts?

Normally, interpretation is conducted in court premises but interpreters do make themselves available to serve the public beyond the courts. For example, in the event that a deponent or person making the affidavit is ill and immobile and has to affirm statements in an affidavit (which at a later stage will be produced by his lawyer in the course of the hearing of the case), the lawyer can seek special permission from the court to have the relevant interpreter taken to the deponent's home. There, the interpreter interprets and explains the contents of the affidavit to the deponent. The affidavit is then permitted to be used in court, having been duly signed by the deponent.

When an accused is arrested but is medically unfit to attend court, the police can seek the court's permission to have the accused remanded in hospital until medical authorities find him fit to be discharged from hospital and able to attend court. In order to remand the accused in a hospital, the procedure calls for a legal judicial officer from the courts, accompanied by a police prosecutor and a court interpreter, to visit the accused at the ward where he is admitted and guarded by the police. Whilst there, the interpreter reads and explains the charge preferred by the police. The legal judicial officer then proceeds to remand the accused in consultation with the police. Interpreters also accompany judicial officers from the courts to read and explain charges to accused persons remanded in prison.

Whenever an election is held in Singapore, interpreters in the three languages – Mandarin, Malay and Tamil – are deployed to the nomination centres. Should any contesting candidate or supporter in his party wish to seek clarification on the election laws, he can seek the assistance of the interpreter assigned to that centre, if the person is not conversant in English.

Interpreters attached to Parliament are also deployed to serve as interpreters at general meetings headed by ministers and members of parliament, such as at the NTUC Delegates Conference, and on special occasions like the May Day Rally when the prime minister addresses the nation. Interpretation in the three major languages is compulsory and simultaneous interpreters of the parliament are deployed.

What happens if a litigant speaks a language other than the official languages provided for in the Constitution, i.e. Mandarin, Malay and Tamil? The State Courts have a list of qualified foreign interpreters, e.g. Thai, Bangladeshi and Vietnamese. These foreign interpreters assist the courts in reading charges and interpreting to foreigners during trials.

If a foreigner needs the services of a foreign interpreter for personal reasons, e.g. to translate a private document like a birth certificate for submission to a government department like the immigration authority, the applicant is referred to a qualified foreign interpreter registered with the State Courts for assistance.

So, a court interpreter not only functions in court premises but he has also to stretch his arms beyond the courts to render a greater level of assistance to the public at large!

MY DREAM — BUT HOW DID I BECOME AN INTERPRETER?

What I should do after my basic education was the question of the day. My father was adamant I should consider continuing my studies. Whether I could pursue studies at tertiary level that involved having to spend large sums of money was the big question the family faced. Despite his meagre salary as a clerical officer at the Telecoms Department, my father insisted he would sponsor my studies.

My family had great hopes that I would make it as a lawyer at all costs. To be a lawyer was my dream too. I had in mind my

In 1964, posing with members of Bartley School's Historical Society.

father's dream. But my dream was a bigger one. It was twofold: To achieve it as a lawyer; and at the same time to become a scriptwriter in Tamil and English, to produce and direct a TV episode or a full movie.

I spent many precious days of my youth imagining myself as a film director. Even after I joined the Judiciary at a pretty young age I travelled all over the country with serious ambitions of producing films. I became so caught up in my thoughts that I pushed the idea of doing law behind me. Totally lost in a world of dreams, I was torn between my two ambitions.

My father and my family.

But what surfaced in my life was a job as a court interpreter after I signed up with the Public Service Commission and accepted it. Why this choice was something I could never understand. One possible reason was that I needed a job, and a regular income. I couldn't bear to see my father struggle to pay for an expensive law course when his income could hardly provide three meals for the five-member family.

Finally came the job

I was absolutely overawed by the fact that I had succeeded in getting a job ... in the courts ... and that too in the Singapore Civil Service. A monthly income of $243.75 was then an unexpectedly large salary that could keep a family of five going. I remembered how I queued up to collect my very first salary – cash in a window envelope that featured my long name and ID particulars!

I recalled how I dutifully handed my first pay packet to my mother and how my mother faithfully placed it at the family altar. I could understand her emotions. The money I brought home supplemented what my father earned. Did that mean we would have more nutritious meals every day? Maybe.

At the courts

On my first day of work, I reported to the Registrar of the District and Magistrate's Courts at South Bridge Road. The two-storey building was old, dilapidated and wore a coat of paint that showed its age ... the exterior certainly never revealed anything majestic. The officer I reported to was an elderly Sikh gentleman, one Mr Randhir Singh.

I was taken to see the rest of the shabby-looking building: the courtrooms – some small and some really large – and other parts of the court building. I met my immediate supervisor. He was a sulky-looking man who seemed to want to show off his great wealth of experience. He spoke non-stop as if he was Mr Know-All. It was a very disappointing first meeting. I was irritated and far from impressed. But I decided to stick it out.

The initial training

In the second week I was placed under two senior officers. It was meant to be an on-the-job training but one officer dumped me in Court No. 9 ... a mentions court, he told me. A disastrous beginning. Later I learnt that anyone charged for a criminal offence would be brought to this large courtroom for first mention, when the charge would be filed formally against him.

It was a place crowded with accused persons, police officers and scores of members of the public who flocked to the courts in support of their loved ones involved in court-related matters. I sat down in a corner to observe my colleagues in action and soon realised that there was a fairly disproportionate number of Indian cases for a community that made up less than six percent of the total population at national level.

I found that most accused persons were from low-income families. Petty thefts and assaults formed a large portion of Indian cases, besides sex-related ones. My very first impression of my fellow Indians was disappointing. I didn't expect Indians to be in such bad shape. But that was the reality of life in those days.

Within a few days I was able to pluck up courage to stand before a crowded courtroom, read charges to accused persons and address the trial judge clearly and confidently. Sooner than I had expected, I developed an interest in my work, encouraged by colleagues who seemed impressed that a fresh schoolboy could have the courage to stand tall and speak eloquently in a full courtroom.

The bonding began

As my immediate colleagues reported well of me to my supervisor, he would occasionally drop by to see me in action. Although a rather fussy and fault-finding person, my supervisor did occasionally share some sentiments of his long experience in the courts. Gradually I took a liking to him; I even tolerated his long sermons of how he had earned a good name as an interpreter and as a supervisor.

He soon paid special attention to my needs. Our relationship improved and he was no longer the man I had disliked at our first meeting. It took us quite a while to understand each other and when we did, we began to enjoy each other's company. He often came with a problem for me to solve or a question to answer. Seeing that I took pains to meet his requests, he visited me regularly.

Under his direction, I began to receive interpretation work from his deputies for assignments outside the main building.

Almost all requests from the Traffic Courts, the Coroners and the Civil District Courts became my assignments. I enjoyed taking the long walks and short bus rides from the main office to the designated courts.

The probationary period and tuition

Placed on a two-year probationary period, I had an examination to sit before being confirmed in the service. So my life was not one of just reading charges in courts but attending language classes as well to prepare for the probationary examination. Three times a week I attended English lessons at Fullerton Building which housed government offices then.

The class was small with fewer than ten trainee interpreters and translators from various government departments. The tutor, a secondary school English teacher, was the man behind our lessons. He brought life to our lessons and was real fun to be with. We enjoyed his guidance, his lessons and more importantly his confidence in us.

The 10.30 tea breaks became something we looked forward to every morning. Occasionally, Mr Eric would join us at the Boat Quay coffee stall and he never failed to spark our discussions, the topics of which were varied. Mr Eric allowed us to share our views freely on almost anything: politics, government policies, open discussions on matters related to youth.

We cannot deny the excitement those tea breaks brought to our lives. Whilst we were considered 'students' in our respective departments, Mr Eric treated us as adults and respected our views and suggestions.

Meanwhile, besides attending classes in English, I had another language to work on. A Tamil interpreter was required to learn, prepare and pass Malayalam in order to be certified.

To prepare me for the exam, it was arranged that I take tuition in Malayalam.

Yet another tutor

My tutor was a Civil Service officer. Mr Narayanan had retired from service but had been recalled to assist the interpreters' group. A native Malayalee, Mr Narayanan was a sought-after interpreter for cases involving the Malayalam language. Under his able tutorship, I developed a keen interest in Malayalam.

Impressed with my keenness in the language, Mr Narayanan enjoyed conducting lessons longer than scheduled. My one-hour lessons soon saw extensions of twenty and thirty minutes. We enjoyed long conversations on a variety of topics – from family issues to the courtrooms, and from cases to current affairs, culture and human behaviour. On some occasions we were so carried away that the discussions went into our lunch breaks.

Motivated by Mr Narayanan, I began to spend a great deal of time reading Malayalam together with Tamil. I was soon able to think in Tamil and Malayalam. At the same time, I was giving serious thought to improving my skills in Malayalam even further as I was going to use it a lot – especially as I would need to take promotional examinations in Malayalam. Together with a colleague who came on board later, we went scouting for a good tutor on whom we could rely to prepare us for professional translation work in Malayalam.

Mr Arunan, our saviour

The search was an exhaustive one and finally we chanced upon a contact at the Malayalee Association situated at 44 Race Course Road. At that time there was a local newspaper, the *Malaysia*

Malayalee, in circulation in Singapore. We had an appointment fixed with its editor who was later to become our tutor, friend and confidant.

At 6pm after work on a Wednesday, my colleague Palani and I went to meet the said editor at the association. After a twenty-minute wait on the ground floor, we were invited to a room on the second floor by a fairly short, serious-faced gentleman whose name we later learnt was Arunan.

All three of us felt comfortable at our first introductory meeting. We were as much impressed with Mr Arunan as a reliable, competent tutor as he was with his two promising lads who would, in the next few months, be his ace students. The enthusiasm that bound us, the drive to prove our mettle and the verve of our youth pushed us all the way to safe grounds.

For a tutor, Mr Arunan spoke very little. Maybe this was because, as an editor, he wrote much more than he spoke. In the next few months we tried translating pieces that stretched our capacity but we were ably guided by Mr Arunan whose expertise as an editor spoke well when we were confronted with extremely difficult terminology in our assignments.

Whilst gratefully acknowledging Mr Arunan's contribution, we cannot forget Mr Narayanan's role. As interpreters, our primary work is oral interpretation during trials. Whilst Mr Narayanan prepared us for the courtroom arena, Mr Arunan laid the foundation for translation of documents and speeches and ensured we were prepared at all times for both forms of translation.

That we were sufficiently trained within the two-year probationary period was credit to our tutors and us, as the trainees who had industriously put in many hours of hard work.

The verve to shine

As trainee interpreters, we had to learn while we work. I was sent from court to court – from the lower courts to the higher courts that dealt with more serious cases, and from the main court building to neighbouring courts: the Traffic Courts, the Juvenile Court, the Civil District Courts, the Coroner's Court, the Syariah Court, etc.

I must confess I was young, energetic and vibrant and it wasn't an issue to travel all over, rain or shine. I enjoyed visiting the courts and meeting different groups of fellow colleagues and handling a variety of cases. I may have shown great enthusiasm in my work as my seniors readily sent me to do trials in hearing courts.

In the beginning I was a little nervous but felt encouraged by colleagues and court staff I worked with. Judges too played an important part in my progress. Inspired by some judges, I developed a keen interest in doing trials. I loved listening to mitigations by defendants. I always felt that mitigation is an important ingredient in a trial.

As such, I took pains listening to defendants in person, collating their thoughts and then presenting a well carved-out piece of mitigation to drive home to the Bench the message that the litigant needed to be given due consideration for what he had said. When given due weightage, this would warrant some amount of leniency when sentence against him was passed.

The death sentence is passed …

Some of you may have attended court sessions out of interest and curiosity. You may have heard certain words or phrases used by the judge just before the prisoner is sentenced for a capital offence. On conviction, the sentence for a capital offence then was none other than death.

When those gathered in the courtroom rise when requested to do so by the Assistant Registrar of the Supreme Court, the following words are read out:

"LET ALL PERSONS PRESENT IN COURT RISE AND REMAIN SILENT WHILE SENTENCE OF DEATH IS PASSED UPON THE PRISONER (PRISONERS)."

Following this, the trial judge goes on to pronounce the death sentence, thus:

"THE SENTENCE OF THE COURT UPON YOU IS THAT YOU BE TAKEN FROM THIS COURT TO A LAWFUL PRISON, AND THEN TO A PLACE OF EXECUTION, AND THAT YOU BE HANGED THERE BY THE NECK UNTIL YOU ARE DEAD."

I have interpreted in several capital offence cases throughout my career. Interpreting the death sentence has never been a pleasant experience for me. At the end of a long trial, which sometimes takes weeks, the conviction will be followed by the verdict – the death sentence!

Many may wonder what the reaction of the prisoner(s) is when the sentence is passed. Some prisoners may tear; some are totally without emotion; some may expect such a decision and therefore stand in the dock staring into space! How had I felt? Often it is a sad feeling. I feel disturbed and moved when explaining the death sentence – but it was a duty after all!

Fortunately the prisoner(s) is whisked away from the dock almost instantly. What is left? Perhaps the cries and woes of the loved ones of the prisoner(s) in the gallery. Quite often it is the mother's uncontrollable emotional outburst – death is always painful!

CASE 1

FIRST APPEARANCE IN COURT
A gruesome gang rape

It was my third year in the courts as an interpreter.

As a young, junior officer I had been trained to do simple cases. My work was mostly reading of charges where I ascertained the plea, conveyed it to the court and explained to the accused the queries, if any, from the Bench. Once the plea was accepted, the facts of the case would be explained to the accused and if he disputed any part of the statement of facts, the prosecution would clarify. If the accused accepted the statement of facts in totality without any qualification, his plea would be fully accepted. If the court was not satisfied that the accused understood the nature and consequence of the plea, the plea of guilt by the defendant might be rejected.

I was completely in the world of a mentions court, reading, explaining and interpreting charges when the defendant spoke only Tamil or Malayalam. The mentions court is a first court in which an accused is charged. Usually, more than fifty cases a day were dealt with, unlike in a trial court where there will only be one case a day set for hearing.

I had not been exposed to a trial until then. I was instructed to assist a senior interpreter in a Preliminary Inquiry. At such an inquiry, the accused person(s) would be charged and the prosecution would lead evidence to establish that a case(s) had been made up.

The magistrate having conduct of the inquiry would, if satisfied that a case had been made out, commit the accused for a full trial in the High Court, at a later date. If it was a capital case, no bail would be offered and the accused person(s) would be remanded in police custody.

I was briefed with the details of the trial by very senior officers. There would be prosecuting officers, defence lawyers, police personnel, the press, etc., I was told.

I received the information with great anxiety and enthusiasm. My first maiden appearance in an inquiry – a rape trial. The experience was going to be new!

Four Indian youths had committed gang rape on two nurses – both Chinese – who had been on night duty in a clinic. The incident had not been met well by the general public and had caused some uneasiness in the community. I observed that after the incident Chinese women would appear uncomfortable when they were amongst Indian men – understandably so, because of that case.

The youths had consumed liquor that rainy night in Sembawang Village. Drunk, they had then gone on a rampage and finally arrived at the clinic which operated twenty-four hours and tended to the needs and medical problems of the village residents.

Two nurses, XL and XO, were on duty.

The ruffians knocked on the door of the clinic. XL (the married nurse) asked XO (the unmarried one) to answer the door. XO had just switched on the lights. One intruder barged in, followed by the other three.

The youths were armed with a knife and other weapons. XO was blindfolded and pushed on to a bed. One of the youths slapped and assaulted her.

XL was also dragged to the same room. She was repeatedly punched despite pleading for mercy, saying that she was a mother of two children. She was threatened with strangulation if she did not allow the accused to have sexual intercourse with her.

This was a grisly rape case that shocked the nation.

Preliminary Inquiry

On the day of the inquiry, I arrived at the courtroom early, tense and emotional. How did I feel when I first saw the four accused persons? As an interpreter, an official of the court, I ought not to feel prejudiced against the accused even though the acts they were alleged to have committed might have been gruesome. After all, the law required that the charge against the accused be proven beyond a doubt.

I looked at the four accused – all youths! They did not appear fierce like the villains in Tamil movies. The four seemed so normal! Could they have committed such a gruesome offence, I asked myself. My first impression was that they were a cheerful lot, chatty and lively, despite being in the dock.

Witnesses were produced; exhibits and documents pertaining to the investigation into the rape were submitted to the trial magistrate, Mr Boey Kun Hong. The two nurses were present in court. The prosecution adduced evidence through them – briefly.

I sat in the courtroom staring at the two nurses! Why did they have to suffer the trauma that they did? Were they not discharging an onerous duty during the night when the rest of the country were peacefully asleep?

I thanked God the nurses were not Tamil-speaking. Would I have been able to interpret for these traumatised witnesses especially after they had been subjected to such brutality?

One could not deny the fact that the two dutiful officers had been manhandled by four sex-hungry hooligans out to satisfy their lust.

The four accused were committed to stand trial for rape, the defence lawyers reserving their rights to cross-examine witnesses at the full trial before the High Court.

The Trial

Some months after the Preliminary Inquiry, I was sent on a three-month training period in the High Court. While there, I was told I would be assigned alongside a very senior colleague, the late Mr P Athisdam my mentor, to interpret in a three-week-long hearing before the late Justice Choor Singh.

I learnt that the High Court hearing was for the same Sembawang rape case. At the time, I was assisting in a murder trial (my first ever in the High Court) but I was ready for the rape case – having already been familiar with the facts of the trial at the Preliminary Inquiry!

Seated in the dock were Gopal Krishnan, aged 23; A Veeraya, aged 19; R Subramaniam, aged 19 and M Tarmar, aged 20. Mr M N Samy appeared for Veeraya and Mr Joe Chellam for Subramaniam. Both Gopal and Tarmar appeared in person, unrepresented by counsel. Mrs Rosalind Quek held a watching brief for the two nurses. Deputy Public Prosecutor (DPP) K S Rajah led evidence for the prosecution.

What was revealed in court by the prosecution in its opening address was truly startling. To quote DPP K S Rajah: "The details of this somewhat tragic scene would make *Lady Chatterley's Lover* look like a nursery rhyme. This is the tale of two women who, like angels of mercy, would have flown or rushed to the aid of ailing mothers and new-born babies."

Senior consultant S N Goon of Kandang Kerbau Hospital who had examined XL told the court how traumatised XL had been, and how it had taken her a long time to answer questions put to her. She finally said she had been raped.

The same consultant told the court that he had also examined XO and it was after prolonged questioning that XO, upset and agitated, admitted that she had been raped.

The doctor also told the trial judge that Ms XO had said she was single and had had no previous sexual experience. Evidence was also adduced that XO's eyes were bruised with congealed blood and these were attributed to injuries caused by clenched fists or multiple blows.

Defence lawyers cross-examined Dr Goon at length as to whether the number of persons who inflicted the injuries had been ascertained. Dr Goon in his reply said categorically that no one could medically state how many persons were involved.

A host of other witnesses were called. The two nurses offered a vivid account of what transpired on the night of the rape. They took the witness stand for a few days. Their stories revealed how the accused persons had planned their attack, how cunningly they had made their intrusion into the clinic, how cruelly they had treated the two helpless nurses, and all the inhumane activities that night.

The two lawyers posed a series of questions in their attempt to break down the key witnesses. The younger nurse, especially, broke down during questioning when lawyers dug into the details of the events that night although, throughout the trial, the judge ensured that the nurses were not overly harassed during cross-examination.

I felt very angry when questions were put to the younger of the two ladies that caused her to break down during questioning by counsel. I could feel her anxiety as she struggled to recall the details of the incident on that fateful day. Must the law allow lawyers to torment the poor witness with such a hurtful, embarrassing line of questioning, I asked myself. I was emotionally disturbed each time the poor lady was questioned.

The accused persons looked much more intimidating when they shared uncalled-for remarks about the victims. What audacity I told myself. But I remembered what my colleagues had cautioned me: "It is not for the interpreter to be judgmental. The accused must be proven guilty and for that to happen the defendant must be accorded a fair hearing. The accused must be heard. There is no reason for the interpreter to be personally attached to the case."

It was clear after the nurses had testified that they had sufficiently cooperated with the DPP to establish that all four accused persons had had their share of cruelty and brutality at the time of the commission of the rape.

The two defendants appearing in person without lawyers spoke in Tamil and tried to put questions to the nurses that absolved them from the offences. Satisfied that the prosecution had established a prima facie case, the trial judge called upon all four accused persons to enter upon their defence.

All four of them spoke in Tamil and I was allowed to interpret for the two defendants with shorter testimonies. One accused pleaded alibi; he testified he had not been at the scene of crime at the time of the incident and called witnesses to confirm the alibi and corroborate his evidence.

As I interpreted the accused's alibi evidence I felt he wasn't telling the truth, but who was I to draw such an inference. The role of the interpreter is to interpret. Inferences are drawn by the learned trial judge and not anyone else.

The defendant's witnesses tried to establish that the defendant was elsewhere at the time of the alleged offences. These witnesses had a tough time convincing the court and I had the difficult task of interpreting their unclear versions. I realised how difficult it was to be an alibi witness – dates and times were crucial and one small slip-up would get the evidence disallowed.

The alibi witness tried to portray a friendly attitude towards me. In between his evidence, the witness tried to convince me that his friend, the accused, was not at the scene of the crime and that the accused ought not to be put through such agony.

The prosecution went all out to totally discredit the accused persons and their witnesses. Reading charges/interpreting facts is altogether a different game, I discovered. Although my senior colleague congratulated me later for a good job done, I could not hide my fears of doing a 'big' trial.

I was extra cautious whenever the trial judge, the late Justice Choor Singh, stared at me through his spectacles. I realised during the long trial that I was able to withstand the 'ordeal' because of the verve I had as a youth – I was then only twenty-one years of age!

I had known before the start of the trial that Judge Singh could be intimidating with his stern looks. I was therefore cautious and well-prepared not to be disturbed by any quarter. Interpret dutifully, thoroughly and conscientiously I shall.

As expected, both the DPP and the lawyers made lengthy submissions. Mr K S Rajah was firm in his remarks that all four accused had their respective roles in the well-planned and carefully executed crime.

He invited the court to disbelieve the defence stories and to give weight to the prosecution's credible evidence. Mr Rajah submitted that the case in question was no ordinary case and if the appropriate punishment was not meted out, rapes may go rampant.

The Verdict

Justice Choor Singh deliberated on the verdict before delivering it on 11 September that year. A total of 84 years and 35 strokes of the cane was meted out as sentence. Other charges were taken into account in passing the sentence.

All four were convicted and sentenced for robbery. They had robbed XL of $10, and $14 and a transistor radio worth $17 from XO. These offences, the court held, were committed when the accused were armed with weapons – knives.

The court took into account that the four accused persons had robbed the nurses of their possessions by holding the victims against their will and in the absence of consent. In taking turns to rape the nurses, the four accused brutally attacked them repeatedly, right up to the wee hours of the morning.

The court considered the immense distress and pain the victims had suffered. The younger of the two ladies had so many injuries that she was later hospitalised.

Over the twenty-six days of hearing, Justice Choor Singh was presented with an overwhelming amount of evidence implying guilt on the part of the accused; they included bloodstained pyjamas, the fingerprints of the accused at the crime scene and confessions.

In sentencing the accused, Judge Choor Singh remarked thus: "The evidence clearly shows that you committed the most despicable crime against helpless ladies. The most violent and serious offence against a woman is the offence of rape.

"I want you and other like-minded hooligans to know that rape, whether organised or not, cannot be tolerated for one moment and will be struck down mercilessly."

This case is especially remembered for the following:

- When Singaporeans came to know of this case, there was much uproar, anger and disbelief. For some time after this case, there was a distance between the Indian and other communities.
- At the time this crime was committed, DNA technology was not available. But the investigation team working industriously round the clock collected items of evidential value – both physical and medical. It was remarkable that the police, without such facilities then available, succeeded in making a strong case against the suspects and charged them in court with the most serious charge – gang rape.
- Something unusual happened during the trial. The trial before Justice Choor Singh turned out to be lengthy. The list of witnesses was long; material witnesses spent a huge amount of time on the witness stand. Throughout the trial the four accused repeatedly told the court, through their counsel and when testifying, that they had been treated with utmost cruelty and threats and that the police had tortured them to record their statements for use against their defence.

They complained of cruelty by the police, particularly by Insp Kalpanath Singh who was the investigating officer in charge. They made allegations that statements obtained by Insp Kalpanath were by means of inducement and threats. As they sat in the dock, the four discussed amongst themselves that the "vicious and cunning" Insp Kalpanath ought to be taught a lesson. They also made remarks about Justice Choor Singh.

Realising after some time through the trial that the prosecution was heading towards securing a conviction, one of the accused picked a convenient moment to throw his slipper at the trial judge when he took the witness stand.

This untoward behaviour was deemed totally unacceptable and the trial judge convicted the accused of contempt of court with an additional three months' jail term.

When the trial ended, and my courtroom ordeal was over, my stint in the High Court also ended. I returned to my workplace in the District Court – back to mentions and reading charges. I could not believe I had interpreted in a mega trial. For days I recalled the trial and spoke to close colleagues about my first experience in the High Court environment! I was convinced I could stay long in the interpreters' service – it turned out to be true, much to my disbelief.

Would I be able to face a stern-looking Judge Singh again? Yes, I am confident after this long trial. Another such criminal case? Why not?

CASE 2

MY FIRST MURDER TRIAL
A man kills his friend

In the early years of my service as an interpreter, I was sent to the High Court on a three-month study tour. One of the reasons for this unexpected arrangement was that my seniors found that I had a keen interest in observing and interpreting in criminal trials in the High Court. I had occasionally gone to the High Court to cover duty and, whenever I was free, I would spend a good deal of time reading notes of evidence on criminal cases. I was particularly interested in submissions made by prosecuting officers and defence counsel.

I was fortunate that during the three-month stint at the High Court, I was asked to assist in a murder case set for trial. By that time, I had sat through a few Preliminary Inquiries in the lower courts and I was familiar with court procedures for a capital case. I was very happy to be assigned the trial.

I still vividly remember this case. The accused was Tamil-speaking and there were a few Tamil-speaking witnesses as well.

It was the first criminal matter, a murder case that would be heard by two judges of the High Court. By an amendment of the law, trial by judges and jury was abolished and replaced by hearing by two judges. It came into effect in January 1970.

The concept of two judges hearing a case was new and the High Court was handling the concept for the first time. A trial in that fashion was undoubtedly new to me – more so as I was to interpret in a murder trial for the first time ever.

In court I learnt for the first time that, in the High Court, the charge is read out by the judge's secretary and interpreted to the accused by the interpreter. The plea is then obtained by the interpreter and duly reverted to the judges.

For the first time, I uttered, "The accused pleads not guilty", in the High Court building.

The accused was one Mohamed Kunjo. The prosecution had led evidence that he had caused the death of the victim. As in all capital cases, a Preliminary Inquiry had been held in the District Court and the case was sent to the High Court for a full hearing. On the evidence presented, a magistrate had committed the accused Mohamed Kunjo for trial in the High Court.

The Trial

On the day of the hearing, I arrived in court early to read up and familiarise myself with the facts of the case. I listened attentively to the DPP's opening address and faithfully interpreted to the accused, Mohamed Kunjo, in the dock. He was a dark-complexioned man, soft-spoken and very serious. He looked around the courtroom as if searching for someone. As I was to interpret the entire prosecution case to him, I sat outside the dock next to him. "Are you well?" he whispered. I looked straight into his eyes and forced a smile to confirm that I was well.

But I suddenly felt unwell seated next to a 'killer'. I couldn't bring myself to accept that the man seated with me had caused the death of his bosom friend. The accused kept looking at me as if wanting to strike a conversation with me. "No private conversations," I told myself. "Will you speak for me? I only speak Tamil," Mohamed Kunjo slowly started. "I am assigned to interpret for you," I replied abruptly, my voice barely audible.

The DPP said in his opening remarks that the accused and the victim were friends and had remained so for almost thirty years at the time of the killing.

The victim had a family in Singapore whereas the accused was a loner here; his family was in India. The victim and his family had accepted the accused as a family member. The evidence unfolded at the trial revealed that the victim's daughter had looked up to the accused as a father figure and had always addressed him "father", with great affection.

Both men worked in the same company and the accused would spend his off days with the victim and his family.

On that fateful day, 25 May 1976, which was a Sunday and a rest day for both men, the two had sat down in the open area of the victim's house to spend the day relaxing. They talked and consumed liquor from as early as ten in the morning. They continued drinking after lunch. By late afternoon, they had consumed quite a bit. Intoxicated, their conversation for the most part was slurred, neither understanding the other. A quarrel broke out and they hurled vulgarities at each other.

They started to hit each other and were soon wrestling on the ground. Suddenly the accused went to a store nearby and picked up the exhaust pipe of a motor vehicle. He then struck the victim on the head with the pipe. The men, both drunk, were staggering about by then. The victim tried to block the blow but almost at once fell to the ground. He lay in a pool of blood and died subsequently. Medical evidence, the DPP said, showed that the victim most probably died of a fractured skull resulting from blows behind the ears.

When the court called the accused to give his evidence, he chose not to give evidence on oath but made an unsworn statement from the dock. In his short statement made under caution, he said the fight between him and the victim started when he told the victim not to drink when driving lorries.

Angered by what the accused said, the victim punched his eye. The accused said the victim also struck his left hand with a piece of wood. The accused said he hit the victim back but could not remember with what. He said he had no intention to kill the victim and did not know that the victim would die.

Mohamed Kunjo's unsworn statement was short. He was repetitive about what had transpired on the day of the killing. He looked at me as he narrated, appearing to seek my sympathy. When he explained how he had struck the victim, he paused and looked towards his counsel. Each time Mohamed slowed down or paused, I became more cautious as I interpreted his statement. The trial judges, both non-conversant in the Tamil language, focused their attention on me. After all I was serving as Mohamed Kunjo's voice.

A doctor who conducted the autopsy gave evidence and was subjected to a prolonged cross-examination by defence counsel, in the course of which he conceded that there was a number of possibilities as to the cause of death, including that of a fall.

He concluded that the fractures on the left forehead occurred after death because they were not associated with any haemorrhage, and gave his opinion that the victim most probably died of a fractured skull resulting from two blows with a blunt instrument behind the ears.

It dawned on me during the trial that I was going to have many such experiences later in my career. Although I had in my working life interpreted in many long criminal trials, this trial always remained special in my mind! Was it because this was the first of many experiences?

The case proceeded for twenty days. Several witnesses, including the victim's wife and daughter, testified. In his defence, the accused narrated the sequence of events that led to the victim's death. His tearful account revealed how much he loved the victim and his family, how grateful he was to the only family that had cared for him throughout his many years of stay in Singapore. He maintained that he had never intended to cause any harm to the victim and that he was too drunk to realise what he was then doing.

The Verdict
The trial judges rejected Mohamed Kunjo's evidence of a sudden fight. They convicted him of murder and pronounced the death sentence! It was a first for me, interpreting the death sentence. Having sat through the trial for twenty days and it being my first trial in the High Court, I was emotionally moved when I interpreted the death sentence. I couldn't believe that I stood there and told an accused that he had been given the death penalty.

The accused showed no emotion; I had sympathised with him and hoped that he would not be given the death penalty but the law had to take its course.

I was troubled for many days. Each time I shared the experience with a close friend or colleague I asked myself whether I should stay on the job. Soon, experience and the courtroom environment got the better of me. I stayed on to do many more capital cases. I not only interpreted the death sentence in a silent courtroom for many more years of my working life, I also visited convicted prisoners in Changi Prison and spent hours with them reading and interpreting the contents of their petitions, pleading for clemency.

The case went before the Court of Criminal Appeal. Mohamed Kunjo appealed against the decision of the two trial judges. It was canvassed on behalf of Mohamed Kunjo that he had not at the time of the incident an intention to cause death.

The Court of Criminal Appeal comprising three judges reviewed the evidence and concluded that there were no grounds at all for changing the conviction of murder. It upheld the decision of the trial judges!

At the time that Mohamed Kunjo's case was heard in the Singapore High Court, appeals were allowed to be sent to the Judicial Committee of the Privy Council in London. (The law in Singapore later did away with the appeals going to the Privy Council. The decision of the Court of Criminal Appeal then became final with no further appeal.)

Three points were canvassed before the Privy Council: (1) the cause of death, (2) whether the appellant Mohamed Kunjo was so intoxicated as to be incapable of forming the intent necessary to constitute the offence of murder, and (3) the defence of sudden fight, which if proved by an accused reduces the offence to one of culpable homicide not amounting to murder!

The Judicial Committee of the Privy Council – a Bench of five judges – heard the appeal after it was dismissed by the Court of Criminal Appeal in Singapore. The judges there agreed with the trial judges and the judges of the Court of Criminal Appeal.

The appeal was duly dismissed by the five-man Bench. The Privy Council judges said categorically that they would not interfere with the trial judges. They agreed with the trial judges who had ruled they had no doubts that the appellant was, at the time of the commission of the offence, capable of forming and actually did form the intent necessary for murder, which finding had been upheld by the Court of Criminal Appeal.

The evidence of the assault showed that the victim had been taken by surprise and attacked with a very unusual and unexpected weapon, a heavy blow on the head which could reasonably be expected to be lethal.

The Privy Council held that in the face of the evidence, the appellant could not show that he had not taken undue advantage or acted in a cruel or unusual manner and therefore there was no need for the trial judges to refer to the defence of sudden fight.

I recalled how the manager of the two men, when he testified at the trial, described the drunken state of both the accused and the victim. Both men had been highly intoxicated before the incident. They had been unable to take instructions to load and deliver timber that night. It was in such a state of drunkenness that the two men had punched and pushed each other before the accused finally struck the victim.

A year later, I was excited to hear that the Privy Council in London had affirmed the decision of the Court of Criminal Appeal in Singapore. However in the last paragraph the Lordshohip stated: "The judges of the Privy Council respectfully drew the attention of those whose duty it was to advise the President on the death sentence, that the offence was committed more than two years ago, and that there were mitigating factors worthy, it may be thought, of consideration before a decision is taken in regard to the sentence."

I separately learned that on his Petition for Clemency, the accused's death sentence was commuted to one of life imprisonment instead.

Young, inexperienced and completely new to the judicial process, I received the news with some jubilation. I felt life imprisonment was more than sufficient punishment for someone who had caused death without any intention whatsoever to do so. Following the finding of the Privy Council, the accused in this instance was given life imprisonment.

The Mohamed Kunjo trial left an impact on me. I kept asking myself how it was that this could happen in a thick friendship that had lasted for years. For the first time I realised that alcohol was a sore point in many Indian families.

I was satisfied with my performance. Although a little unsure of myself at the start of the trial, I believe I had spoken clearly whilst interpreting. Counsel for the defendant thanked me for my services. He said I had done a good job interpreting for his client.

I felt motivated, this being my first ever capital case in the High Court. I later asked my colleague who paired with me in the case for his comments on my performance. "You did fairly well and spoke with confidence. It would have been better if you had looked up to the Bench when you addressed the court. You are almost there," he said.

CASE 3

ONE OF MY EARLIER MURDER TRIALS
A drinking session turns ugly

Yet again another scene of violence, another stabbing, another loss of life. The root cause was consumption of liquor. That alcohol had often been the basis of a criminal trial has often upset me.

I was always excited to interpret in capital cases. All capital cases were transferred to the High Court for a full hearing although mentioned for the first time in the Subordinate Courts. The Preliminary Inquiries of these capital cases were also heard in the Subordinate Courts but the trials were heard in the High Court. The lower courts heard non-capital cases such as theft, cheating and causing hurt. Having come from the lower courts, a junior officer like me was all excited, craving to hear the different aspects of law in a criminal trial. Reading up notes on the case before the opening of the trial was not a necessary feature but I found great interest in doing that.

The case I was assigned to was a murder trial before judges A P Rajah and Choor Singh. I was to work with a colleague. As usual the hearing was set for three weeks and the norm was that I, being a less experienced officer, would spend most part of the trial seated next to the accused person. In practice, I would do the opening: interpret to the accused the murder charge that was read out in court in English by one of the judges' secretaries, and then interpret the plea from the accused (usually 'not guilty' in the case of capital charges), to the court.

From then I would be seated next to the accused person throughout the prosecution's case, diligently interpreting to the accused the evidence as led by the State. Often the evidence was that of medical experts like doctors who had examined the injuries inflicted on the victim after the offence was committed or who had examined the accused whilst in police custody, the autopsy report of the State pathologist, etc. Such evidence would be followed by that of material witnesses: the eye-witness' account, evidence of witnesses corroborating such account, police officers' accounts, especially that of the investigating officer.

Evidence of other police officers too would be led by the prosecution. During a hearing the prosecution might introduce a statement(s) made by the accused to the police. If the accused had mentioned in his statement(s) matters contrary to what he was then saying in his evidence in court, the court would conduct a process called a trial within a trial. This proceeding is called a *voir dire*. In this process, the accused takes the witness stand and is put to a test of his credibility. He has to explain the content of his statement(s) and be subject to cross-examination by the learned deputy prosecutor.

I have never been comfortable sitting through a *voir dire*. The interpretation of this part of the trial can be lengthy and exhaustive depending on how much discrepancy there is. In some cases, the defence will fight tooth and nail to have the accused's statement(s) – which had been recorded by the emforcement agency such as the police, CNB, etc. – thrown out on the ground that the defendant had been forced to give the statement either under some threat or a promise/inducement.

At the end of a *voir dire*, the trial judge will decide if the statement can be admitted. If admitted, the accused will have more to explain. If the result of the *voir dire* works in favour of the accused, the accused will stand a better chance of clearing himself of the charge over his head when the court invites him to state his defence at a later stage. But if at the close of the prosecution case the court is satisfied that the prosecution has made out a case, the accused will need to adduce evidence on his part in order that he would not be convicted.

It is also my duty to interpret for the accused when he later chooses to testify. This may again be lengthy because the accused needs to give satisfactory explanation to the judge(s) on very pertinent issues raised by the prosecution which, if not done, will tilt the case in the accused's disfavour. Should the accused call witness(es) to substantiate his evidence, I will interpret for such witness(es) as well. Of course my colleague working with me on the case will come to my aid if I become tired at the witness stand.

The Trial

In the dock was one Visuvanathan charged with murdering a Madikum Pushpanathan on 23 January 1976 at 7pm. The venue of the incident was a bar at the junction of Jalan Besar and Upper Weld Road. Leading the evidence for the prosecution was DPP Sant Singh. A B Netto was counsel for the defence.

It was the prosecution's case that, at the material time, the accused and the victim were drinking liquor at the bar. The accused became aggressive and challenged the victim to a fight. Other patrons at the bar separated the two. The accused however pulled the victim by his hand to the road. There he started a fight. In the course of the fight the accused pulled out a knife he had concealed, stabbed the victim in the chest and ran away. The victim collapsed on the road and died in a pool of blood.

The pathologist conducting the autopsy found a fatal gaping stab wound below the victim's left clavicle. The cause of death was certified as 'stab wound into the heart'. It was contended that if the accused's act of stabbing was done with the intention of causing injury and the bodily injury intended to be inflicted was sufficient in the ordinary course of nature to cause death, he was guilty of murder.

Defence counsel submitted that there was no evidence that the accused inflicted the fatal wound with the intention of causing such injury as would, in the ordinary course of nature, cause death. The trial judges convicted the accused, explaining that there was a clear distinction between the intention to cause bodily injury found to be present and the intention to cause 'some bodily injury of a kind which is sufficient in the ordinary course of nature to cause death.'

The State produced witnesses who were present outside the bar at the time of the stabbing, friends of the accused and the victim. My colleague at the witness stand had much interpreting to do. Speaking in Tamil, witnesses gave contradicting evidence as to the actual events at the time of the incident. The prosecution led evidence through them as to the details of the fight between the accused and the victim and the manner in which the knife was used in the cause of the fight.

Realising that several witnesses directly involved in the fight were to be called to the stand to testify, my colleague and I decided to share the translation work. Having gone through the Preliminary Inquiry notes before the hearing, we decided that we would, as much as possible, use the terms employed by the police translators during the recording of the statement(s) to the police. The witnesses therefore did not have an opportunity to find fault with any of the interpreters.

In his defence, the accused used the term "swinging the knife". He offered an explanation and insisted my interpretation was not what he had wanted to say. The trial judges sought clarification and stood by my interpretation.

Cross-examining these witnesses, the defence tried to establish that the accused did not inflict the fatal wound. The defence also questioned the witnesses as to how well they could have seen the fight in the dimly lit area outside the bar after 7pm.

It certainly wasn't easy interpreting for witnesses with different versions of the same incident. Most often, the witnesses were unable to recall the sequence of events. If one said the area was brightly lit and good enough to see the stabbing clearly, another would say otherwise. The witnesses also contradicted themselves: the statements they gave in court differed in part from their earlier statements!

It turned out to be a fairly long trial because of several witnesses being called.

The Verdict
The judges said they had no doubt that the fatal injury caused by the accused on the victim, using the knife, was an intended injury and was not caused accidentally or otherwise unintentionally. It was in their opinion also sufficient in the ordinary course of nature to cause death.

The judges remarked – having regard to the weapon used, the force used in stabbing the victim, and the fact that the victim was stabbed in a very vulnerable part of his body – that they had no doubt at all that the accused had an intention to cause the victim's death. They recounted that the accused had used a kitchen knife for cutting vegetables and inflicted a fatal gaping stab wound below the victim's left clavicle.

The force used was such that it caused an 8-cm deep wound and the blade of the knife had cut through the third and fourth ribs, penetrated the left lung near the anterior margin of the left upper lobe and then produced a 2-cm cut on the anterior surface of the heart.

Testifying, the accused said that he was swinging the knife wildly from side to side in order to defend himself. The trial judges were convinced that there was no doubt at all that the accused, when he stabbed the victim with the kitchen knife, intended to cause some bodily injury to the victim of a kind sufficient in the ordinary course of nature to cause death.

Each time I hear of such an incident – a stabbing or a fight – I will hope it's not another drink episode! Drink ruins the happiness of many Indian homes. Sad it is but true to the core!

There is a Tamil saying that "Drink destroys the home." Alcohol has for many decades been the root cause of unhappiness between spouses and caused emotional hurt in children – particularly when they witness unpleasant scenes in the home. Arguments between a husband and wife can land one party in the hospital or both parties before a tribunal, mediator or a counsellor. Many a husband being referred for alcoholic treatment is not uncommon!

CASE 4

DELIVERING THE DEATH VERDICT
A father's love ends in tragedy

Before my transfer to the High Court in 1976, when I was assigned to a mentions court, I once read a charge of murder to an elderly Indian. Within weeks, when the accused was produced in the same court for a further mention of the case, I observed that he had greyed very much.

I saw for myself the effect of a murder charge hanging over an accused's head. The accused in this case, N Govindasamy, had been emotionally wrecked by the pending charge.

The Facts
The victim, Mohamed Azad, a Muslim, was at the date of his death on 16 November a young man aged 29. He had graduated from the University of Singapore in 1968, and at the time of his death, Mohamed was employed as an executive at Singapore Airlines.

In 1971, Mohamed came to know a Hindu girl, Deva Kumari, who was then a second-year student at the University of Singapore. She was the third child of the accused, N Govindasamy, who owned a packing and transport business.

Before Deva Kumari met Mohamed, she had been estranged from her father, the accused, and had in October 1970 left her family home in Kerbau Road and taken up residence at Eusoff College at the university campus.

Some time in 1972, Mohamed and Deva Kumari became secretly engaged. The couple had plans to get married after Deva's graduation. Deva's parents did not know of the engagement, neither did they know of the couple's intention to get married. Mohamed never visited Deva's parents at their home in Kerbau Road and she never introduced Mohamed to her parents, even as a friend.

Deva moved to a hostel in Lloyd Road in 1974 in her final year of university. During that time, the accused's wife was away in India, and the accused would send food that he had cooked to Deva at her hostel on weekends. Some weekends Deva would go back to the Kerbau home for meals.

One evening in 1974, Deva and Mohamed returned to the hostel at about 11pm and were surprised to find the accused and his youngest daughter waiting for Deva. This was the first time her father had seen Mohamed. On seeing Deva, he accused her of associating with a lot of men and asked her who Mohamed was.

The accused met up with Deva a few days later and apologised to her for his behaviour. He asked Deva to resume going home for lunch during the weekends. Deva told her father who Mohamed was, and his place of work. Despite her father's pleadings, she continued to refuse to go home for lunch.

There was an arrangement for Mohamed to meet her father to pick up a diary at Kerbau Road. Deva however told Mohamed that she did not keep a diary and that it would be crazy of Mohamed to go to her father's house for that purpose.

Accepting Deva's advice, Mohamed said he would arrange to meet her father at Tivoli Coffee House instead. Mohamed later told Deva that as her father could not leave the house, Mohamed would meet him at Kerbau Road.

Mohamed had planned to meet and dine with Deva and two of his close friends at 7.30pm at Shangri-La Hotel. When Mohamed did not show up as planned, attempts were made to locate him. Calls were made to the accused's home. Mohamed's friend, Arunachalam, decided to drive to Kerbau Road.

There, the accused informed Arunachalam that Mohamed had been there to collect a book and left at 5pm after a drink. As Mohamed failed to show up, Arunachalam made a formal report at the police station that Mohamed was missing.

As a result of the formal report, the police interviewed the accused and recorded two statements. In his statements, the accused spoke of his concern for Deva, the circumstances which had led to her leaving home to stay on her own, Deva's refusal to come home for lunch despite the accused's pleas for Deva to do so, the accused's questioning as to who Mohamed was and the relationship between Deva and Mohamed.

The accused also said in his statement that he had given Mohamed a book entitled *Which Religion?* that touched on children's problems and the different practices of the various religions.

On 21 November 1974, a gunny sack with a human foot protruding from it was found floating in the sea near a jetty at Kallang. According to the pathologist who performed the post-mortem, a chopper found by the police at Kerbau Road had been used to cause seven injuries on the victim.

The same pathologist confirmed that all the seven head injuries were caused by downward blows, four of which were inflicted from behind the victim.

In his two cautioned statements, the accused told of a fight: how both had fallen during the struggle, how the accused had seen a chopper but did not know how he had used it. The accused touched on the topic of religion discussed between the accused and the victim.

Mohamed had spoken of his religion and insulted that of the accused. The accused had become angry and scolded him. Angry, Mohamed had punched the accused who retaliated. Both fell to the ground. There the accused saw the chopper. He said he did not know how he used it. The accused also said that, not knowing what to do, he disposed of the body.

The Trial
During the trial before two judges in the High Court, the accused chose to make a statement from the dock, in his defence. The accused gave an account of what transpired in his home at Kerbau Road on the fateful day. He therefore gave the State no chance to cross-examine him on his accord of the killing.

The accused said he was shocked when Mohamed told him that he was going to marry Deva. This angered him and he had moved towards Mohamed who punched him. There was an exchange of blows. The accused got hold of the chopper and slashed Mohamed. When the accused came to his senses, he said he found Mohamed slumped by the chair.

In his defence, the accused claimed grave and sudden provocation. He pleaded similarly before the Court of Appeal, i.e. that the deceased had started the fight, hurting him with strong language, humiliating the Hindu religion and its practices.

The Verdict
The Court of Appeal rejected his defence of grave and sudden provocation. They found that the appellant had inflicted the seven fatal wounds found in the head of the deceased with the intention of causing his death.

The case of N Govindasamy was indeed rare in that two lives were lost because of a father's fear of losing his daughter to a man professing a totally different religion from his.

The facts of the case clearly reveal a man's strong conviction for a religion he adored against another's and how deeply rooted religious beliefs work and to what extent a father would go towards protecting a daughter he loved.

CASE 5

A CHARGE OF CULPABLE HOMICIDE
Spousal killing

The High Court has seen many different kinds of people in the dock charged with capital offences. Not always are the persons accused of murder wanted criminals. The ordinary layman too can face a charge of murder if circumstances take control of him.

A split second decision to cause grievous hurt to another can, if the element of intention is proven, land one with a murder charge. Anger, fury, uncontrollable stress, emotion, revenge – almost everything and anything can give rise to causing a death!

In the next episode of murder, we meet a young police inspector who, in a fit of rage, caused the death of his wife, a police corporal. The date of the incident is 17 August 1982. The young officer was charged not with a capital charge, but with one of culpable homicide not amounting to murder.

The Trial
The prosecution's evidence showed that the accused, his wife (the deceased, Madam Lim Quek Kim), his 14-year-old stepson Henry and their natural daughter Sheila were staying in the police quarters at Queensway. The marriage between the accused and his wife had not been a happy one largely owing to the unfaithfulness of the accused who had several affairs outside the marriage.

At about 11.30pm on 16 August 1982, after the accused had returned home, a heated argument broke out between the accused and his wife. The cause of the serious quarrel was love bites which Madam Lim found on the accused's neck. She continued to question the accused about the love bites. The quarrels between them resumed in the master bedroom and Henry heard sounds of someone being punched.

Henry then heard a loud noise, followed by a muffled one. He heard the accused say over the phone, "This is an emergency ... come quick ..." The accused gave his address in full over the phone. In another call Henry heard the accused say, "I believe my wife is dead, please come quick." The police radio division received a message at 0114 hours on 17 August 1982 from the accused who said "dead ... dead". The accused telephoned his superior and, identifying himself as Inspector Selvaraj, said "I have killed my wife."

Forensic pathologist Prof Chao examined the deceased at the scene at 0230 hours and ascertained that death had occurred within two hours of his examination. An autopsy carried out on the same morning certified that the cause of death was asphyxia from smothering.

Having heard the prosecution, Justice Lai Kew Chai called upon the accused to enter his defence. The accused testified that Madam Lim had charged at him, attempting to claw out his eyes. To prevent her from attacking him further, the accused said he rained blows on Madam Lim who fell face down. She was groaning and crying in pain. The accused later found her dead.

The accused had earlier given a statement to the police. His version in court was similar to the statement made to the police.

In that statement, the accused said that his wife had continued to abuse him with vulgar language in their room.

He had asked his wife not to raise her voice for fear that the neighbours could hear them, and he had thrown a pillow at her to quieten her. But his wife had charged at him and the two had had a scuffle. She had attacked him and in retaliation the accused said he had delivered some punches. She had fallen on to the bed and begun to groan. When he later approached her to console her, there was no response. He noticed his wife frothing from the mouth.

The accused called expert forensic pathologist Dr Dharamvir to testify on his behalf. Dr Dharamvir offered the opinion that Madam Lim could have suffered concussion and could have asphyxiated accidentally.

The Verdict

The court convicted the accused as charged. The trial judge was satisfied that the victim had not concussed or asphyxiated accidentally. The court also held that the accused did smother Madam Lim to death, knowing that his act of smothering would be likely to cause her death. The accused was accordingly convicted. The court took into account the mitigating factors and imposed a sentence of eight years' imprisonment.

The judge commented on the evidence of the accused's stepson, Henry. He ruled that there was no contradiction at all. There were discrepancies, but mostly minor. The judge observed that Henry's evidence on the second and fateful day, including the two screams and what followed thereafter, remained unshaken.

It must be observed here that the court gave weight to the evidence of a young person and relied on his evidence compared to other witnesses called by the State. Henry was a mere 14-year-old lad but the trial judge found his testimony more reliable and believable.

Henry was a material witness for the police in this case. What if he had testified in Tamil? It would have been a challenge for me handling an underaged witness but Henry spoke in English. All the same, I stood by Henry in the event he needed any assistance whilst testifying.

Commenting on the testimony of the accused, the judge said he formed the impression that the accused was a person who knew police investigation procedures rather well and was capable of providing evidence to explain what he had done or said.

As an example, the judge said to explain away his statement to the ambulance officer that Madam Lim had taken something, the accused had said that he thought she had taken sleeping pills.

To support his allegation that the froth found in the mouth of the deceased was like stout foam, the accused had suggested that Madam Lim had drunk the stout in the refrigerator – this the court held was a complete fabrication. Also, knowing that Madam Lim had asphyxiated, the accused chose to tell his superintendent that his punches had killed his wife!

The case involved a trained police officer – an Inspector – an officer of rigorous training in many fields: physical, mental and psychological. Yet all his knowledge and exposure could not help him beat the law. He failed in his effort to convince the court. The trial judge was able to read through him – the testimony of the accused failed to impress the trial judge who concluded that the accused had fabricated relevant portions of his testimony.

Although I wasn't directly involved in interpreting in the trial (none of the witnesses spoke in Tamil), I sat through the entire trial observing with keen interest submissions made by defence counsel on why the case in totality did not warrant a severe punishment.

The accused, having admitted in his statement to the police (which he repeated in his testimony in court) that he had on the fateful day inflicted the injury which caused his wife's death, led the trial judge to call upon him to enter his defence. The defence did not make any submission that the prosecution had not made out its case.

It left defence counsel Mr Pala Krishnan little to offer in the accused's favour. Nonetheless, counsel impressed upon the court carefully canvassed points contributing to mitigation on behalf of the accused. Counsel invited the court to consider the accused person's contribution in his role as a law enforcement officer, and traced the history of events on that fateful day, pleading for utmost leniency on behalf of the accused.

Counsel submitted that the accused and Madam Lim had had a good family life until she became overly suspicious of the accused's association with other women. The victim, counsel submitted, had often questioned the accused about love bites she had spotted on him whenever he returned home in the night.

The accused, it was submitted, was unable to withstand his wife's constant nightly nagging. Quarrels, and often the use of violence, became a regular feature in their home before the incident on that fateful day, 17 August 1982, the culmination of emotional outburst over many months of suspicion and ill-feeling.

The trial judge considered the mitigating factors rendered by counsel and ordered an eight years' imprisonment term!

I felt a custodial sentence was appropriate for what the accused had done. The victim nevertheless was provocative but the accused need not have behaved in such a ruthless and rash manner.

CASE 6

ANOTHER CASE OF ALCOHOL-RELATED DEATH
Passion takes the better of them

Almost every murder case involving an Indian revolves around a state of drunkenness. Often the accused is a fairly young man who, in a state of intoxication, inflicts a severe injury that ends in the death of another young man. Usually the victim is a good friend or close colleague. A long friendly session of pleasurable drinks that leads to an incident, a fight, bloodshed and the death of someone who never deserved it!

Some time in 1988 there was a trial before two judges in the High Court. It took me a while before I convinced my conscience that it was my duty – if assigned – to perform with a clear mind, unprejudiced. I reminded myself that the accused was merely charged at that stage – the case against him needed to be proven beyond a reasonable doubt! Even if it revolved around alcohol, what if the accused was guiltless?

In the dock was a fairly young Indian, a Malaysian, working in Singapore. The evidence led by the State was that the accused, the victim Neelamegam and two other workers (Muniandy and Rajendran) shared the same cubicle in their quarters at a construction site. One day all four men sat down to drink and play cards. A quarrel developed between the accused and the victim, with the accused saying he was going to stab the victim.

He was seen picking up a knife, catching hold of the victim and stabbing him three times. An ambulance was summoned but it was too late – the ambulance attendant pronounced the victim dead. On arrival at the scene, the police stated that the accused's breath smelt of alcohol. But the accused could walk steadily without support; neither did he fall asleep or vomit in the police car.

At the CID, the accused gave his statements. He later claimed that none of the statements he made were voluntary. The accused contended that because he was intoxicated, he was not able to form the intention to inflict the injuries that caused the death of the victim.

Evidence led by the prosecution was that, on the morning of 30 November 1987, the accused, the victim and the other two left for work, returning after 9.10pm. The victim (Neelamegam) was cooking dinner whilst the others took turns to bathe. The accused was the last to bathe. Meanwhile he had given Muniandy $10 to buy drinks. Muniandy bought a big bottle of ABC stout, a can of ABC stout and a small bottle of wine.

They began to drink at about 10.25pm. The accused consumed the big bottle of ABC stout. Rajendran and the victim shared the wine; Muniandy consumed the can of stout. The four men then sat down to play cards – a game called *thuroop*. Rajendran partnered the accused. There was a quarrel as to the winning team, both claiming victory. However, soon the quarrel stopped and they went on to play a second game.

In the midst of the game, the accused got up and helped himself to some food. Seeing this the victim asked the accused, "Are you going to play with a hand soiled with curry?" This started a quarrel between the accused and the victim. The other two suggested calling off the game as the drinks were almost all consumed, but the accused and the victim continued their quarrel for another twenty minutes.

Muniandy was having his meal on the floor. The accused scolded him, asking how it was that the victim had mixed up all the cards. There was a further quarrel between them. At that point the accused was heard to say that he would stab the victim. Rajendran saw the accused take a knife from the rack, whilst holding the victim with his left arm. The accused then stabbed the victim twice on the left shoulder.

Rajendran quickly ran towards the accused who by then had stabbed the victim a third time. Rajendran caught hold of the accused's right hand but he refused to drop the knife. Rajendran had to punch the accused three times before he could wrench the knife from the accused. An ambulance was summoned.

When the ambulance attendant reached the cubicle, the victim was lying on his back with the accused lying next to him. When persuaded to move, the accused did so on his own without any difficulty. The ambulance attendant said the accused swayed from side to side and smelt of alcohol.

The ambulance attendant heard the accused say in Tamil, "I stabbed him with a knife. I stabbed him in anger." According to Rajendran, the accused had scolded him, "You were the one who took the knife from me. Your fingerprints are on the knife. You are also involved. You punched me and Muniandy is a witness."

The Trial

A trial within a trial to determine the admissibility of the four statements was held. The accused's main complaint was that he had not given the statements voluntarily. He accused the Inspector and the CID interpreter, Mrs Jayaletchumi, of obtaining the statements under inducement or promise. The Inspector was alleged to have told the accused through Mrs

Jaya that if the accused should admit the offence, the accused would receive a reduced sentence.

The accused also alleged that the Inspector had repeatedly warned him to tell the truth. He also accused Mrs Jaya as having told him, "You better tell the truth." Both the Inspector and Mrs Jaya emphatically denied that any promise or inducement had been uttered in the course of their recording of the four statements.

It is not uncommon for accused persons to allege that the police offered promises or inducement in the course of recording statement(s) from them. When such an allegation is made, the court must conduct a proceeding called *voir dire*, "a trial within a trial". Police witnesses are called to the stand to explain how the police recorded the statement(s).

In this instance, the accused challenged the statements he had made to the police, and took on the investigating officer and the police translator who had interpreted for him during the recording. I listened carefully and closely watched the accused testify for fear that he may at a later stage find fault with my interpretation. However the trial judges ruled that there was no element of threat or inducement and that the accused had volunteered the statements.

The trial within a trial was extensively long. There were four statements – and the accused vehemently challenged the admissibility of all the statements. My colleague and I were kept busy throughout the trial. The accused, speaking in Tamil, told the trial judges through us all that he had to say about the role of both the Inspector and Mrs Jaya who had served as the interpreter for the recording of the four statements. Besides the accused, the material witnesses for the prosecution too required the services of Tamil interpreters.

In addition to accusing the Inspector and Mrs Jaya of procuring inducement or promise, the accused also contended that it was because of intoxication that he was not able to form the intention to cause the victim's death. The trial judges, convicting the accused of culpable homicide not amounting to murder, held that:

1. The fact that a police officer reminded a witness that he should tell the truth and not tell lies could not constitute a threat or an inducement.
2. In some cases 'you better tell the truth' could amount to a threat or an inducement. But in the circumstances of the present case, the words did not suggest to the accused that he would gain any advantage by giving the statement.
3. The investigating officer had administered the warning for s 122 (5) of the Criminal Procedure Code (which related to the admissibility of statement/s by the accused) on the first occasion, but not on the subsequent occasions. However, on the subsequent occasions, it was not necessary to repeat the warning as it was a continuation of the first statement.

The trial judges added, "... this is an unfortunate incident. The two of them, who were obviously fellow workers, and who shared a cubicle with two others, allowed their passion to have the better of them. To our mind, this was due in no small part to the liquor they had consumed. A tiny misunderstanding was blown out of all proportions. The two had quarrelled before but their previous quarrels had apparently never reached the nasty stage like the present instance where physical violence was resorted to. Accordingly, we find the accused guilty of the offence of culpable homicide not amounting to murder."

The trial itself was a fairly short one but the trial within a trial took a few days. The defence fought hard to maintain the accused's stand that the incident happened because the accused was intoxicated and did not know the extent of the injury he had caused.

Once again alcohol had played a lead role in the lives of the victim and the accused in this episode where a state of drunkenness had led to a fight, and death!

Will the Indian community overcome this problem? Only time can tell!

CASE 7

A DIFFICULT AND CHALLENGING TRIAL
The result of uncontrollable anger

In December 1990, a killing took place at a carpark that was a short walk from a popular Hindu temple in Serangoon North. The Dharma Muneeswaran Temple has been in existence for many years now and faithfully serves a large Hindu population not only in the Serangoon area and its precincts, but a larger area covering Ang Mo Kio and the nearby Hougang housing estates. I frequent the temple and never fail to visit it at least once a week!

It is twenty-seven years since the incident took place. Even now, I feel uncomfortable when I walk past the block of flats and the coffeeshop on the way to the temple.

The coffeeshop is fairly large. It is popular with regular temple goers; devotees visiting the temple will stop by for a drink or a meal on the way home after prayers. A variety of Indian, Chinese and Malay food is available.

As many brands of beer are sold at the coffeeshop, groups of foreign workers and youths who live in the vicinity gather there late at night over beer sessions. The regular groups on occasion stay past midnight. Fist fights amongst drinkers are not uncommon.

The Trial
Nadunjalian s/o Rajoo was charged with the murder of

one Ambalagan s/o Rathanan at the car park beside Block 111, Serangoon North Ave 1, at about 9pm on or about 17 December 1990.

When we were first assigned to cover the case, my colleague and I read through the available notes and familiarised ourselves with the evidence that would be unfolded at the hearing. Not to be caught off-guard, we went through an exhaustive glossary of vulgar and abusive terms such as "fellow without testicles", "mother fucker", "pariah son", "pubic hair fellow" and "son of a cunt" that we expected to come up in the trial. An interpreter must at all times be sufficiently prepared to face difficult situations in a trial.

The accused at the time of the killing was twenty-one years of age. The victim, a friend of the accused, was twenty-five years of age. The accused and the victim would often go for rides together on the victim's motorcycle.

There were three eyewitnesses to the incident – all were mutual friends of both the accused and the victim. They would meet from time to time at the coffeeshop situated at Block 107, Serangoon North Ave 1, and have drinks together.

Before that fateful day, the accused had heard from a friend that the victim had called the accused "a fellow without testicles" – meaning a coward. On the day of the incident, the accused went to the coffeeshop for a drink and a meal. The victim joined the accused some time later.

The accused testified that they chatted for a while before he confronted the victim with what he had said. To that the victim replied abusively, saying "no-dah, mother fucker". Shortly thereafter, three other friends joined them. When all five were at the table, the accused calmly asked the victim about the abusive words that he had spoken.

The victim remained silent. A few seconds later, he told the accused to follow him as he needed to talk to him. The other three friends also left the coffeeshop and followed the victim and the accused.

The three eyewitnesses gave similar accounts of what happened next. By that time, the five had reached a PUB substation near by. Soon there was a fight between the accused and the victim. The eyewitnesses testified that they saw the accused stab the victim and that the victim's back was bleeding.

They tried to hold the accused back. In the meanwhile, the victim walked away in pain but the accused ran after him, pushed him to the ground, sat on him and continued to stab him. All four of them then went home separately, leaving the victim lying on the ground.

The victim was found with serious injuries and sent to Tan Tock Seng Hospital where he was pronounced dead at 10.25pm. The forensic pathologist who performed the autopsy testified that the victim had twenty-four wounds all over his body and the cause of death was haemorrhage from multiple stab wounds.

In the course of the prosecution's case, a statement that was earlier recorded from the accused was introduced by the Deputy Public Prosecutor. The prosecution contended that the statement was recorded without any threat, inducement or promise.

Defence counsel later withdrew his objection to the admissibility of the statement and the statement was therefore admitted. The accused was accordingly called upon to enter his defence.

In his defence, the accused said that he loved his mother dearly, particularly after the separation of his parents. He added that, as a Hindu, he regarded his mother as God. He testified that on the night of the incident, he had left the table after the heated exchange of words and he had no weapons with him. He then heard the victim murmuring "fellow without testicles; son of a cunt". The victim then glared at the accused and said "pubic hair fellow".

At the substation where they later stood facing each other, the victim pointed a finger at the accused and continued, "Pariah, son of a cunt; pariah, son of a prostitute." Incensed and infuriated by the victim's remark that he (the accused) had had sex with his (the accused's) mother, the accused punched him. A fight ensued. The victim then said, "I will not leave you without killing you today" and thrust a knife towards the chest of the accused.

The accused managed to grab the knife from the victim. He started stabbing the victim in fury. The accused said he was furious because the victim had insulted his mother, calling her a prostitute.

The witnesses in this case were quite liberal with their use of foul language and abusive words. Much depended on my colleague's and my interpretation. Words such as "mother fucker", "fellow without testicles", "pubic hair fellow" and "pariah, son of a cunt" needed much guidance. On occasion when the accused questioned our interpretation, the court stood by our explanation and saw the case through smoothly.

At the time that the case was being heard in the High Court, the temple devotees somehow learnt that I was involved in it and they approached me to find out the stage of the trial. Often I told the devotees to look up reports in the newspapers for the latest on the case.

I recall one evening at the temple when an elderly devotee walked up to me to enquire if the accused would be hanged. "This is a cruel act. It is murder. Please see to it that the 'naughty' accused is sent to the gallows," she said. Surprised, I looked at her and said, "The court will see to it that justice is meted out."

The Verdict

After a two-week trial, the trial judge found the accused guilty of the killing based on the evidence the prosecution had against the accused. The accused appealed against the judge's finding of guilt. Lawyers Leo Fernando and Suchitra Ragupathy of Leo Fernando represented him at the appeal before the three judges of the Court of Criminal Appeal.

The Appeal Court dismissed the appeal and upheld the single trial judge's decision of guilty of murder. The findings of the three judges were based on the following: the forensic pathologist's evidence that there had been twenty-four stab wounds, of which the fatal ones were of sufficient brutality to cause the death of the victim; the accused's admission at the trial that he had stabbed the victim; the evidence of the three eyewitnesses that the accused had not only stabbed the victim repeatedly but had also run after him to stab him further despite their efforts to restrain him.

For many months after the incident, devotees congregating at the temple never failed to discuss the incident and the gruesome killing. I must confess that many of them attending prayers at the temple continued to feel eerie, especially whilst walking home at night towards the main road.

This case is particularly remembered for the amount of interpretation work involved. There was a host of witnesses who testified, many speaking in Tamil. The *voir dire* (trial within a trial to establish the voluntariness of the accused's statement) lasted many hours.

The prosecution had a tough time cracking the accused in the process of establishing the voluntariness of the statement made to the police. The accused had an equally difficult task clarifying his stand.

Interpreting for a witness, and especially an accused person, on the credibility of statements made by him to the police in the course of investigation is always a difficult and challenging experience for an interpreter. The accused person may not be altogether truthful but one must accept the fact that statements are made under very compelling situations.

There is every possibility that the accused could have inadvertently omitted mention of matters which became questionable in the course of his testifying in the trial! I sit back now to recall how difficult a task it must have been then.

CASE 8

"YOU INTERPRET WITH SO MUCH CONFIDENCE."
The failed conspiracy

Not always do the High Court judges try accused persons for murder, armed robbery, kidnapping and rape. In between capital cases, charges of conspiracy to cause grievous hurt do occasionally come up for hearing before the puisne judges.

One such case made its presence some time in 1990 and involved a newspaper distributor. The victim was P Ramasamy, then aged 64. He was the chairman and chief executive officer of the National Co-operative Federation.

At the time, more than thirty years ago, *The Straits Times* and other major language papers in Singapore were distributed door-to-door. Those were the days when bookshops and newsstands were rare. Reliable distributors were the substitutes of the day.

The newsagents and newspaper vendors were mainly Indians. The newspaper business was lucrative and newsagents guarded their areas of distribution jealously. Whenever a vendor had to go away, for example, to make an annual trip home to his family (vendors were mainly from Tamil Nadu in South India), the vendor would arrange for a substitute to cover his area and this substitute would be either a close relative or a close associate of his.

The vendors, because of their long period of service in a particular area, would be familiar with most of the households they served, and these households would address them by name. When households wanted certain magazines or some special news items, they would make specific requests to the vendors who would make it a point to deliver the items to their doorstep as expeditiously as possible.

Occasionally, suspicion and jealousy would arise amongst the newspaper distributors. Such was the case with a popular newspaper distributor in the Serangoon-Thomson-Bartley area named Sinniah Pillay.

Sinniah had a brother, Retnasamy, who died in 1967. Subsequently, Sinniah was appointed co-administrator of Retnasamy's estate. Retnasamy's wife, Kasiammal, was co-administratix. A dispute arose when Sinniah claimed to be entitled to certain business operations of Retnasamy. This led the parties to civil litigation.

The court dismissed Sinniah's claim and he was ordered to pay damages. Sinniah was removed as a co-administrator of the estate and Ramasamy was appointed in his place. Sinniah felt that it was Ramasamy who had instigated his sister-in-law against him. In December 1984, Sinniah decided to take revenge and teach Ramasamy a lesson.

Around that time, one Raja Ratnam was supplying labourers for the newspaper distribution business of Sinniah. The two became close friends. Sinniah confided to Raja Ratnam his personal and financial problems. He told Raja Ratnam that Ramasamy had made his life miserable. Sinniah asked Raja Ratnam for help to organise a group of people "to break a hand or leg" of Ramasamy and send him to hospital.

After Sinniah had spoken to Raja Ratnam of his request to "break a hand or a leg" of Ramasamy and send him to hospital, Raja Ratnam gathered several men to execute the plan.

On 4 July 1985 at about 8am, Gangadaran – one of the men charged – drove a car to a spot near where Ramasamy lived. Another man, Vellusamy, came down from the car. At about 10.07am, when Ramasamy came out of his residence, Vellusamy threw acid at him. Ramasamy died ten days later. Senior forensic pathologist Professor Chao certified that Ramasamy died as a result of the acid thrown on him.

The Trial
Sinniah Pillay was charged that, "you, between December 1984 and 4 July 1985, in Singapore, did engage with one Muhundan a/l K Kumaran, one Pitchay Rajoo, one K Gangadaran, one Vellusamy s/o Vellingappan, one Shanmuganathan a/l S Neelakandan, one Lopez Joseph Benny, one Stephen Raja Ratnam and one Lopez Xavier Legong Benny in a conspiracy to commit grievous hurt to one Ramasamy s/o Packrisamy and in pursuance of that conspiracy and in order to the doing of that thing, an act took place on 4 July 1985 at Taman Permata, Singapore, to wit, a quantity of formic acid was splashed on the said Ramasamy s/o Packrisamy by one or more of you, which act caused severe burns to his person resulting in his death, and you have thereby abetted the commission of an offence under section 326 of the Penal Code (Cap 224) which act was committed in consequences of his abetment and you have thereby committed an offence punishable under S109 read with S326 of the same code."

The prosecution led evidence that after Sinniah had spoken to Raja Ratnam of his request, Raja Ratnam gathered the assistance of all others mentioned in the charge to "break a hand or a leg" of Ramasamy and send him to hospital.

Evidence revealed that having instructed Raja Ratnam to cause grievous hurt to Ramasamy, Sinniah had kept in touch with Raja Ratnam constantly to find out what had been done to Ramasamy.

The material witnesses testified in the Tamil language. "Must break his hand or leg" was the phrase repeated throughout the trial. It was in order to achieve this that the entire group of accused persons, working as a team of conspiracy, planned and executed the act to cause grievous bodily harm.

The phrase needed explanation and the court was told that although the phrase referred to causing hurt to a hand or leg of the victim, its full meaning was to cause severe harm, such harm as will decapacitate the person. Here it would be apt to interpret that the accused Sinniah did not literally mean breaking a leg or a hand but causing severe bodily injury.

Raja Ratnam testified for the prosecution. He admitted procuring the services of others to injure Ramasamy. However he denied that the use of acid was ever mentioned. He said in court that he was shocked to hear that acid had been used. He told the court that Sinniah was also shocked to learn that acid had been used.

The prosecutor put to him that the Tamil idiomatic expression 'must break his hand or leg' meant to cause hurt – serious hurt. He agreed with the prosecutor that the expression had nothing to do with the means by which grievous hurt would be caused.

The prosecution's second witness was Lopez Joseph. His evidence differed from that of Raja Ratnam in two material aspects. Raja Ratnam had testified that Sinniah knew of the acid attack only on 5 July 1985. Lopez Joseph testified that Sinniah had known of the acid attack on 4 July 1985.

Sinniah had met accused persons Rajoo, Vellusamy, Shanmuganathan, Muhundan, Lopez Xavier and Lopez Joseph at Coronation Plaza that afternoon. That Sinniah was present there on 4 July 1985 was also confirmed by Lopez Xavier, the prosecution's third witness.

The second area where Lopez Joseph's evidence differed from that of Raja Ratnam's was in respect of Sinniah's reaction when told of the acid attack on Ramasamy. Lopez Joseph said Sinniah Pillay was not sad, not worried to learn of the acid attack. He said maybe this was because Sinniah was happy that the job had been carried out. When asked how he got that impression, witness answered that he had looked at Sinniah's face.

At the end of the prosecution's case, Mr Gilbert Gray QC, who appeared for Sinniah Pillay as his counsel, submitted that his client Sinniah had no case to meet on the charge. Mr Gray conceded that the prosecution had established that Sinniah was a party to the conspiracy to commit grievous hurt to Ramasamy but there was no evidence that Sinniah wanted acid to be thrown on Ramasamy.

The prosecution however submitted that based on the evidence of its witnesses, it was clear that Sinniah was well aware that acid was to be used to attack Ramasamy and that he was a party to the conspiracy.

Having heard the submissions, the trial judge rejected the submission tendered by Mr Gray on behalf of Sinniah and accordingly called upon Sinniah Pillay to enter upon his defence. The courses open to the accused to enter his defence were explained to Sinniah Pillay in Tamil.

The Verdict

Sinniah Pillay sought the court's leave to consult his counsel. He then chose to remain silent, i.e. he offered no evidence on his part to refute the evidence tendered by the prosecution. After a lengthy mitigation wherein counsel Mr Gray had many good remarks about Mr Sinniah in his private life and a glowing account of the industrious nature of Sinniah in building his newspaper distribution business, Sinniah was found guilty, convicted and sentenced to a term of imprisonment of ten years.

Sinniah appealed against his conviction and sentence. Mr Gray appeared for him and submitted that Sinniah (the appellant) had engaged a few people to inflict injury to Ramasamy. Splashing acid on Ramasamy was never contemplated, Mr Gray argued. Counsel argued that the idiomatic Tamil expression could not be extended to cover the use of acid.

The High Court judges hearing the appeal commented on the trial judge's decision. The trial judge had said that in his view, there was sufficient evidence to show that Sinniah Pillay knew or would have known that the assailants would use acid to cause grievous hurt to Ramasamy. There was evidence that Vellusamy had already bought the acid in Johor.

The trial judge said there was further evidence that after the incident, in the afternoon of 4 July, the appellant had done nothing to dissociate himself from the deed perpetrated by the assailants. The trial judge had pointed out that Sinniah was satisfied that the assailants had caused grievous hurt to Ramasamy and paid them for their role, and obliged the assailants when they asked for more money.

It was reasonable for the trial judge to have drawn the inference that the appellant knew that acid would be used. The trial judge also had pointed out the two versions – the impression as seen by witnesses Raja Ratnam and Lopez Joseph when Sinniah learnt that acid had been thrown at Ramasamy.

Raja Ratnam had said Sinniah was surprised when told that acid had been thrown at Ramasamy. In the case of Lopez Joseph, the court was told that Sinniah did not feel surprised to learn that acid had been used on Ramasamy.

The defence raised several points before the Court of Appeal. Counsel submitted that Sinniah Pillay had been charged under a different section as compared to the others. The trial judge explained that it was the prerogative of the prosecution to decide the charge it would prefer.

Another issue defence counsel raised before the Appellate was that Sinniah had, when called to enter his defence, chosen to remain silent and he ought to be shown leniency. It was explained that, because the appellant had pleaded not guilty, the prosecution had to conduct a full trial before a conviction was entered. The court said the credit given for a plea of guilty in sentencing did not apply to the appellant in this instance.

The defence also raised that the appellant's sentence of imprisonment was not backdated. The court ruled that the power of court to backdate a sentence is a discretionary power. It was further said that the trial judge did not err in not giving the appellant a discount on the custodial sentence.

In all, the case of Sinniah Pillay was an eye-opener for those who believed that the arm of the law could not reach one if the offender in the forefront was one paid to perform the act. Perhaps money does wonders! But is it always true?

Sinniah Pillay's aim was to seek revenge on his enemy, His cruel thoughts saw no limits. The acid ended his enemy's life!

One morning, some time into the hearing of the case and before the court convened, defence counsel Mr Gray QC who represented accused Sinniah Pillay spoke with me. "I have been observing you the last few days. I must admit I don't follow Tamil at all. But I admire the manner in which you pick up the questions whether from the Bench or the lawyers. You digest the question and obtain the witness's answer; you then interpret it with so much confidence. How long have you been in this field if I may ask... I love watching you speak – you are clear and precise. It's a pity I don't know the language. I wish you well young man."

At the end of the trial, in his final address, Mr Gray thanked the court and all parties involved. He particularly expressed his gratitude to me: "My Lord, may I be allowed to thank the learned interpreter. He is simply marvellous."

Now, forty years later, when I recall this incident, it makes me extremely happy that I had done my job with a great amount of passion and discharged my duty with sincerity and utmost professionalism.

CASE 9

A KILLING IN MY NEIGHBOURHOOD
The case of a triangular love affair

Six-year-old Sagaynathan was a primary one student at Jagoh Primary School. His home was at Block 45, Telok Blangah Drive, a short walk from his school. One Tuesday afternoon in January 1991, the little boy was heading home after crossing the overhead bridge along Telok Blangah Road when a woman approached him. She was a familiar face to him. She shared some nice words and, holding his hand, volunteered to accompany him to his flat. Merrily the young boy chatted and walked with her towards his home.

At about 2.35pm, a passer-by found Sagaynathan's body at the foot of Block 45, and immediately informed police at the Telok Blangah Neighbourhood Police Post. The boy's school bag and drink container were recovered at the landing between the ninth and tenth storeys of the block.

The pathologist's examination revealed that Sagaynathan had suffered facial injuries and a fractured elbow. Police immediately began investigations. The identity of the woman was established after several persons in the neighbourhood volunteered information, having seen the boy and a woman not long before the boy's body was found. Investigations led to the apprehension of a woman in Yishun.

Reporters from the press gathered more information about the dead boy and the female suspect. The suspect was named as Kathiza Ammal, aged twenty-two years. She was the lover and cousin of one Gunasekran (Guna). But Guna was also courting the boy's mother, Regina, a divorcee. Kathiza had been infuriated when she learnt of Guna's intention to marry Regina. This hatred, anger and infuriation for Regina led Kathiza to form the intention to kill the boy, Sagaynathan, in order to seek revenge on Guna and Regina.

The Trial
Kathiza Ammal was charged with the murder of six-year-old Sagaynathan by throwing him down the block with force, over the parapet wall. The prosecution led evidence of a triangular love story which ultimately led to hatred and anger, and finally the intention to cause death. The relationship was a complicated one, the prosecution established.

The twenty-six-year-old Guna and his cousin had been lovers before Guna turned his attention to Regina, of whom he began to grow fond. Both women were also having affairs with other men while they were seeing Guna.

Kathiza visited Guna's family home often. She was aware of the actual time Sagaynathan would return from school. On the day of the killing, Kathiza waited for the boy to finish school and walk home. She lured him away, treating him with a cake and a canned drink. She walked the boy to Block 45 and, at the tenth storey, after some hesitation, forcefully pushed the boy over the parapet wall.

Witnesses for the prosecution included three residents of Block 45 who had seen the boy with an Indian woman along the corridors of the tenth and eleventh floors that day. Two other witnesses to whom Kathiza had admitted throwing the boy, were also produced as witnesses.

The material witnesses chose to testify in Tamil, their evidence going mainly towards establishing the family circumstances of Guna, and his association with Regina and Kathiza. Touching on the triangular love affair, the prosecution insisted that the throwing of the boy from the tenth storey was driven by a desire for revenge on the boy's mother, Regina, and was deliberated and pre-meditated.

Relating that the tragedy arose from Kathiza's intimate relationship with Guna, the prosecution traced the events which clearly indicated Kathiza's feelings when she learnt that Regina had been impregnated by Guna.

Satisfied that the prosecution had made out a case for the defence to answer, the trial judge called upon the accused to enter into her defence. Defence counsel B J Lean told Judge S Rajendran that the defence would rely on medical evidence. He said Kathiza was mentally ill and did not know the full extent of what she did when she committed the offence. Counsel sought an adjournment of the trial in order to have Kathiza assessed by an independent psychiatrist. The judge granted the adjournment.

When the court resumed hearing, counsel called the psychiatrist as a defence witness. The doctor tendered a psychiatric report on his evaluation of Kathiza. He explained to the trial judge that based on his assessment, Kathiza was unaware of her action when she threw the boy from the tenth storey on the day in question.

In short, the defence submitted that the defendant was mentally ill and as such the charge of murder could not stand. The prosecution sought court's leave to call rebuttal evidence. The psychiatrist who had assessed Kathiza earlier in the trial, was allowed to re-assess the defendant in view of the defence argument that Kathiza was mentally ill. Between them, the two psychiatrists took a few days at the witness stand.

In his final submission, the prosecutor urged the trial judge to convict Kathiza on murder. He argued vehemently, tracing the events leading to the death of Sagaynathan and highlighting the triangular love affair coupled with the prosecution psychiatrist's assessments, that it was clear that the defendant had caused the boy's death for revenge and that Kathiza's action was deliberate and pre-meditated.

Submitting for the defence, counsel relied on the expert's evidence that Kathiza was, at the time of the offence, suffering from a mental impairment. Citing past cases of similar nature, counsel urged the court not to convict Kathiza on a charge of murder due to her mental condition.

Interpreting for Kathiza was quite challenging. She was slow in grasping questions and equally slow in her explanations. She was later in the trial said to be of low mental ability.

The Verdict

Judge S Rajendran took some time to study the submissions and the psychiatrists' reports before giving his decision. The court reduced the charge of murder to manslaughter and Kathiza was sentenced to life imprisonment.

During the time of the trial, I was a resident in the Telok Blangah constituency. I lived not too far away from Block 45, where the boy's killing had taken place. Almost daily I had to pass the block on my way to and from the main road.

The victim was a student of Jagoh Primary School, a school popular with parents living in that part of Telok Blangah. At the material time, I was an active member of the school's advisory committee. It was inevitable that Sagaynathan's death was brought up at the committee's meeting. Whenever I attended meetings at Jagoh Primary School, the teaching staff had questions about the killing of the student and the progress of the case in court. I avoided the subject as much as I could.

Many residents and shopkeepers in the neighbourhood began to give me strange looks when they heard that the case was being heard in the courts where I was working. Sagaynathan's death became a talk of the area for quite some time.

That an innocent child had to sacrifice his life because of the absurd, unnecessary doing of three irresponsible adults was certainly unacceptable and unforgivable. It is said that love is blind. Can it justify the actions of the trio, Kathiza, Regina and Guna?

All three parties concerned in this triangular love affair were fairly young and may not have realised what they were heading for, blinded by lust more than love. If the parties had been alert and sought guidance and advice from relevant agencies, perhaps the tragedy and all the accompanying emotional pain and stress could have been averted!

CASE 10

INTERPRETING AN UNFAMILIAR ACCENT
A careless woman pays

A man met a woman by chance. She was walking along Hampshire Road near the Farrer Park football fields and the swimming pool. After a brief conversation, the man learnt that the woman was leaving for India the day after. He introduced himself as a police officer from the Criminal Investigation Department and flashed a card as identification. He demanded her particulars. She handed him her passport. He then asked her to board his van to be taken for investigation. She did so to avoid being handcuffed.

After driving for some time, he stopped the van and asked the woman to move to the rear of the van. The woman began to get suspicious of him. He pulled her saree and the strings of her petticoat. She was not wearing a panty. He ordered her to remove her blouse and bra. She did so. When she was naked, he made her perform oral sex. Then he raped her. There was no evidence of violence. Material evidence revealed no sign of injury on either of them.

After raping her, he handed the woman her clothes. The man noticed a knot at one end of the saree. He undid it and found $6,000. He took the money. She then spotted a card attached to a flower basket in the van. She kept the card. On it was a vehicle number – YG 1496. She later confirmed it was the same number as on the licence plate of the vehicle. The man drove off.

Stranded on the road, the woman flagged for help from passing vehicles. One Simon Tay and his wife stopped to pick her up and send her to a police station because she kept uttering "police", unable to communicate in English. She was able to give the vehicle number YG 1496M to the police. The police later ascertained that the man worked as a delivery driver, delivering gifts for Noel Gifts. He therefore had the keys to the van and had full control of the vehicle.

The Trial
The man, Victor Rajoo s/o A Pitchay Muthu, was arrested and charged with five counts: abduction of the female, rape on the female, carnal intercourse with the female against the order of nature, robbery of monies in the possession of the female, and a simple theft.

The accused pleaded guilty to the amended charge of theft whilst claiming trial to the remaining four charges.

The prosecution relied heavily on the evidence of the woman who testified in Tamil. She told the court she had been walking along Hampshire Road on the day of the incident when the accused struck a conversation with her, made her board his van and how the events as spelt out in the charges had transpired.

Although Tamilians from South India generally speak Tamil, people from different villages and districts in Tamil Nadu speak the language with different accents. The words and phrases also differ from village to village.

The victim in this instance basically spoke clear Tamil but resorted to the use of some words unfamiliar to the Singaporean context. Interpretation of the victim's evidence therefore was not easy and straightforward. I had to clarify several words with the accused before an interpretation could be made!

A Tamil-speaking police officer who had assisted the investigating officer in recording statements from the victim alerted me at the start of the case that the victim spoke clear Tamil but would deliberately resort to using unfamiliar colloquial words to deceive the police in the conduct of their investigation. He warned me that I ought to be careful with the said victim when she testified in court.

Alerted, I was extra cautious when interpreting for the said victim. She was quick to learn that we in Singapore spoke a slightly different form of Tamil from hers. The witness chose to use words Singaporean Tamils were quite unfamiliar with. She played with words and terms that confused me, denying them when clarified. I sought the court's permission to check and clarify with the witness before interpreting to the Bench. The victim therefore could not 'wriggle' her way out.

The prosecution sought to admit two statements recorded from the accused on 24 January 1995 and 25 January 1995. The accused challenged the admissibility of the said statements. A *voir dire* or trial within a trial was conducted. Prosecution witness, interpreter Ms Jayaletchumi of the CID, testified that the statements from the accused were recorded without any threat, inducement or promise and that no one else was present when the statements were recorded.

The accused challenged that the statements made by him were not interpreted or recorded as he had stated. At the end of the *voir dire* the judge allowed the statements of the accused as made voluntarily.

At the close of the prosecution's case, the defence was called. The accused narrated his version of the meeting: how he met the victim, where and how he picked her up, how she went into his van, how she readily undressed and willingly consented to suck his penis and how she picked up a cloth, wiped his penis and performed oral sex. The accused denied he had told the victim he was a policeman. He said that what he had said was, "What if I were a policeman?"

At the conclusion of the case, the trial judge observed that the evidence of the accused was challenged by the DPP, but remained very largely intact after lengthy cross-examination. The judge concluded that having carefully scrutinised the evidence of both the accused and the victim, and the manner in which each of them gave their evidence, he was minded to accept the evidence of the accused as being closer to the truth.

The trial judge was satisfied that the forty-four-year-old woman was a mature person (the accused was only twenty-seven-years old). Being a businesswoman, she would know her way around Singapore, having been here several times previously. If she claimed she could not read, why did she in the first place ask to see the accused's identification card, the judge summed up.

Having interpreted for the victim, it appeared very much in my mind (as later summed up by the Bench) that the victim was a mature person, familiar with the Singapore lifestyle and had not been close to the truth when testifying in court.

The judge said he was unable to accept her explanation on the profits she could make out of her business. The court found it remarkable that she did not know the name of the person (a woman) to whom she had sold sarees on credit during her previous trip to Singapore. Neither did she appear at all concerned when she was told that that woman had left Singapore.

The judge found that no weapon had been used. Neither was there a single scratch on either the accused or the woman. It was also observed that the woman had not put up any resistance when raped. On the whole, the judge said it had not only created a doubt in his mind that the woman did not consent to travel in the accused's van or to the sexual acts, but he was convinced that in all probability she did consent.

The Verdict

The accused was acquitted of the first and third charges, the prosecution failing to prove that the victim was abducted for illicit sexual intercourse or that the accused had sexual intercourse with the woman without her consent. The second charge of rape was reduced to oral sex. The accused had himself admitted that the act of oral sex took place and as such was convicted of the second charge and sentenced to a term of six months' imprisonment plus a fine of $2,000.

As for the fourth charge of robbery, the judge said there was no evidence of threat of death or hurt or wrongful restraint in relation to the removal of the money from the woman at the material time. From the evidence, the trial judge concluded it was an act of simple theft. The robbery charge was reduced to one of simple theft. The accused was convicted and sentenced to two years' imprisonment. To the fifth charge of simple theft, which the accused had pleaded guilty to at the start of the trial, he was sentenced to a term of two years' imprisonment.

The DPP appealed against the trial judge's decision. The Court of Appeal considered three main issues: first, whether at the material time the woman had been induced by deception on the part of the accused to travel in the accused's van; secondly whether the woman had consented to having sexual intercourse with the accused; and thirdly, whether the accused had put the woman in any fear of hurt to herself when the accused took the sum of $6,000 from her by force.

In cases of such nature, there obviously would be a conflict between the evidence of the complainant and the accused. The trial judge would have had the benefit of seeing and hearing the complainant and the accused testifying in court. The judge was therefore able to make findings of fact based on the credibility of their evidence. As such, due regard would be given to the findings of the trial judge. The Court of Appeal affirmed the verdict of the trial judge.

The Court of Appeal does not usually reverse the verdict of the trial judge's decision unless there is a need to do so. A trial judge, when he hears a case, has the benefit of seeing and hearing witness(es) testifying before him. As such the Court of Appeal seldom reverses the trial judge's decision. The Court of Appeal judges merely hear the argument of lawyers; they do not get to see witnesses testifying. Therefore they do not get to observe the demeanour of the witness(es).

This case was indeed peculiar. It is not uncommon to see women from India on the pretext of a social visit here make some fast money or indulge in some illicit business. They make themselves available for sex in exchange for money but local men preying on these unfortunate characters are also prevalent.

I wonder how many more Victor Rajoos are operative in our Indian community.

CASE 11

A SUCCESSFUL APPEAL
Everyone deserves a fair trial

I quite remember this case – a murder trial heard by the late Justice Lai Kew Chai. The death occurred, according to the prosecution, on 17 April 1995 between 12pm and 3pm. The venue was a vacant plot of land off Jalan Ulu Sembawang. The accused, Nadasan Chandra Secharan, was arrested on 20 April 1995, charged and convicted in the High Court for the murder of one Ramipiran Kannickasparry. It was revealed in the prosecution's evidence that the accused and the deceased were distant relatives by marriage and they were having an affair.

At the start of the trial, I was informed that I was to be transferred out of the High Court to the Subordinate Courts from where I had originally come, having served twenty years in the High Court. It is needless to say I was keen to see through the trial before my transfer!

The trial was probably the first to be conducted in a Technology Court. There was the question of establishing the skid marks found on a cement patch at the scene of the crime and of proving, from DNA analysis, that the tooth fragment found in the van came from the deceased.

The Trial
Walking into the courtroom I saw a packed audience in the gallery. There were one or two known faces amongst them.

Some waved to me; some held their hands together in greeting.

Soon the accused was ushered in by the prison authorities. He was a small, fair, handsome man. He flashed a broad smile. Taking his seat near mine, Nadasan greeted me, *"Vanakkam Aiya"* (Greetings, Sir). I responded, greeting him back. I was astonished that Nadasan looked so cheerful. He enquired of my well-being, at the same time waving to relatives in the gallery.

The prosecution alleged that on 17 April 1995, the accused left the club where he worked at about 12pm to meet Ramipiran Kannickasparry at her workplace in Ang Mo Kio.

It was the prosecution's contention that Ramipiran wanted to sever her ties with the accused and he therefore had a motive to murder her.

The accused was supposed to have fetched her from her workplace to the scene of the crime. A colleague of Ramipiran's had testified that she was last seen alive at about 12.15pm on 17 April 1995.

The prosecution alleged that at the scene of the crime, the accused ran his van over Ramipiran's body and returned to the club. After his day's work, the accused then proceeded to the Balasubramaniam Temple. Here Nadasan attempted to wash his van clean of any 'incriminating' evidence at a makeshift garage he had.

There were two points Nadasan had to clear in his evidence. A tooth fragment and some jewellery had been found in the van. Assuming that there was sufficient evidence to convict him, Nadasan offered a reasonable explanation for the possible presence of the tooth fragment in the van.

There were instances in the past when the accused and Ramipiran had met inside the van for meals and drinks and she had a habit of using her teeth to open bottle caps. There was a possibility that a tooth could have broken off on such an occasion.

As to the presence of some jewellery items in the van, Nadasan explained that his van was used by various people to attend weddings and that jewellery items were transported on such occasions. Nadasan further explained that the jewellery items could have been present in the van either because Ramipiran had lost them there or they had been dropped by other people who used the van.

He denied having met Ramipiran on the day she was murdered. He claimed that he usually went home for lunch. On that day, he had left the club at about 12.15pm and was on his way home for lunch when his van broke down.

He subsequently got out of his van to look for the fault and repair it. By the time he finished the repair, it was already 1.45pm, and he proceeded back to work instead. In fact, his supervisor Max Foo (Foo), had paged for him at 1.38pm that afternoon and it was undisputed that he returned the pager call.

The accused said that he had called from a telephone at the nearest HDB block and told Foo of his problem with his van. Foo then asked if the accused needed help, but he declined it and said he was able to repair it himself. Foo confirmed what the accused said.

After returning to his workplace at the club, the accused said that he made a telephone call from a nearby canteen to his wife just before 3pm to tell her why he did not go home for lunch.

That same evening, the accused said that he went to the Balasubramaniam Temple at Canberra Road after work at 5pm. He explained that, although his hours of work were between 6am and 3pm, he had to do overtime practically every day. The accused had a makeshift garage at the temple, and he claimed that he went there because he wanted to check his van once more.

After he had tuned his engine and changed a filter, he proceeded to wash his van because it was oily and dirty due to the repairs done earlier that afternoon. He sprayed water on the whole van and wiped the exterior and driver's cabin with a piece of cloth. He proceeded home at about 6.05pm, after having coffee and chatting with the priests and musicians at the temple.

Nadasan took the witness stand boldly and spoke clearly, trying to match the prosecution's questions.

Interpreting Nadasan was no problem. He was clear and took his time to answer questions put to him carefully. When the questions were long, Nadasan politely asked for questions to be repeated slowly. His answers were concise. After the lunch break Nadasan thanked me for being patient with him. He complimented me for speaking Tamil well. He told me he had asked God to have him released. God, he said, was always there for him.

The Verdict

The trial court was satisfied with the prosecution's evidence. It was convinced that Nadasan had carefully planned the murder – that he had brought Ramipiran to the vacant land with the intention of killing her and did so successfully by running his van over her.

Nadasan however remained confident of his innocence. A devout Hindu who annually went to the hills in South India to fulfil his vows, Nadasan had unshakeable faith in God. Besides fulfilling vows by climbing hills in South India, he regularly participated in the fire-walking ceremony conducted annually at the Sri Mariamman Temple at South Bridge Road and observed fasts in line with his prayers.

Refusing to accept the decision of the High Court, he went on an appeal before the Court of Criminal Appeal comprising three judges.

That the accused was prepared to challenge the trial judge's decision in the Court of Criminal Appeal did not come as a surprise to me. Throughout the more than three-week trial, Nadasan had appeared calm. He smiled occasionally and nodded his head as if in disbelief when prosecution witnesses testified – much of the evidence pointing to him, the accused, as the culprit. I later learnt that Nadasan was very confident that he would finally be acquitted no matter how much the prosecution's evidence pointed to him as the killer because, whilst in prison awaiting 'execution' during the appeal, Nadasan had had a vision – a Hindu deity of whom Nadasan was fond, had appeared before him to assure Nadasan that all would be well!

Almost every day of the trial, the gallery was crowded. Members of Nadasan's family and close associates never failed to visit him in court. Some came for the morning session; some came in the afternoon. There were very close ones who showed up every day to give Nadasan the moral support that he very much needed!

Defence Counsel Subhas Anandan took on the appeal as he felt that Nadasan, although the prime suspect, had insisted on his innocence. In the words of Subhas, "Everyone deserves a fair trial and I wanted to give him that."

The Court of Appeal observed:

"On the totality of the expert evidence adduced, we are not satisfied that the prosecution had proved adequately that the tooth fragment originated from the deceased ... Every failure to observe the procedure stated in the validation paper would, in our view, affect the weight to be attributed to the expert evidence unless there were other independent sources to verify and confirm that such departure did not affect the reliability of the findings."

The technical aspects of the case, especially the skid marks of the tyres which the prosecution held was the cause of Ramipiran's death, were thoroughly argued in favour of Nadasan.

The Court of Appeal's three judges unanimously allowed the appeal and acquitted Nadasan of the murder.

CASE 12

ONE OF MY LONGEST TRIALS
An unusual unlawful assembly

Among the few restaurants and drinking joints along Prinsep Street near Cathay Cinema is an area popular with drinkers – a meeting corner frequented by Indians and drinkers of other races and nationalities. It is where Mohican's Pub is situated and the area is usually quiet except for the intermittent boisterous behaviour of some drinkers that 'pollute' the stillness of the night.

On 20 October 2001, a couple of incidents occurred in the early hours. An argument between two groups took place followed by a full-blown fight between a group which gathered at Mohican's Pub, and the staff of the pub. The police arriving at the scene to investigate the incidents picked up wooden poles, knives and an ice pick. As a result of extensive police investigations, arrests were made and charges preferred against eight persons.

I had, after a twenty-year stint in the High Court, just then been transferred back to the Subordinate Courts. At the Subordinate Courts, I served the Family Court. After capital cases in the High Court, family issues – maintenance, divorce, application for Personal Protection Orders, mediations, etc. – were a totally different experience. In 2002, it was yet another phase of work as I was moved from the Family Court scenario to the Subordinate Courts which heard criminal and civil matters.

Somehow civil matters did not interest me as much as criminal cases. Whilst doing several hearings in the civil courts and mentions in the criminal courts (and occasionally criminal trials – some as short as one or two days), I was told of a criminal trial hearing that was expected to be lengthy. Since the trial involved several accused persons and a variety of witnesses, most of whom would testify in Tamil, I was assigned together with a colleague to handle the case. The assignment took me by surprise but I was happy to be handed this case. I had not interpreted in a long trial since leaving the High Court. My last involvement in a capital case had been in 1996.

The Trial

As always, I arrived in District Court No 8 very early on the first day of the trial. The gallery was full of supporters from Mohican's Pub as well as friends and family members of the accused persons. There appeared to be more police personnel present in the courtroom than usual. Reporters and pressmen too were in larger numbers than usual. The eight accused persons, all Indians, appeared friendly and cheerful. They were Md Anverdeen Basheer Ahmad, Rupesh Kumar, Rajendran s/o Rajagopal, Sambalingam T, Natarajan s/o Chinnaiah, Retnam Mohandas, Perumal Naidu Surendra Sean Clinton and Manogaran s/o Amirpan Ramaiah.

As the accused persons took their seats in the dock, one of them, who appeared rather familiar, looked in my direction and smiled. Suddenly he waved at me. "Hello brother, you don't recognise me? Clinton lah, Sir, from the same primary school long time ago," he said. It was the seventh accused, Sean Clinton. I tried to recall but had difficulty placing the said Sean. What struck me was that, if I knew Sean as he claimed I did, I ought not to interpret the case. I discussed it with his counsel and the two Deputy Public Prosecutors (DPPs) in charge of the case. All parties felt that as Sean was English-speaking, I was not expected to interpret for him. As such there was no need to discharge myself. I therefore proceeded with my assignment. I later learnt that Sean had attended the same school as I did during my early primary school years.

> Soon, counsel for the defendants arrived:
> Mr Kannan (for Anverdeen and Perumal Naidu Surendra)
> Mr N Sreenivasan (for Sambalingam and Rupesh Kumar)
> Mr Rakesh Vasu with Ms Gomez (for Rajendran s/o Rajagopal)
> Mr Tangavelu and Mr Shanker (for Natarajan s/o Chinnaiah)
> Mr Jayakumar (for Retnam Mohandas and Manogaran)

Conducting the prosecution were DPPs Tan Wen Hsien and APP Santhra Aiyyasamy. The trial was before the learned District Judge Roy Grenville Neighbour. Perhaps this was the first trial for me before Mr Neighbour in the District Courts. I had interpreted in cases in the High Court previously when Mr Neighbour represented the State as a DPP.

The DPPs opened their case.

Why the fight that night? What was the dispute?

On the night of 19 October 2001, with the exception of Rupesh, the other accused persons met at the Jalan Berseh Food Centre (JBFC) for a drinking session. At 3.00am the next day, Anverdeen, Rajendran and Sean Clinton went to Mohican's Pub at Prinsep Street for more drinks but were not served. They left the pub feeling disappointed and unhappy.

When the defendants were called to enter their defence, they all denied the charges against them. Each accused had an explanation for his involvement in the events of the morning of 20 October 2001. All eight accused persons denied any form of violence on their part. They also denied being armed.

In brief they told the court they had gathered at the JBFC for a drinking session. After some time, they proceeded to Mohican's Pub. There they were denied drinks. Subsequently the cars they were in were stopped by police officers. They alleged the police officers were rude when they asked the accused for their identification. The court was told of a scuffle outside the pub involving from ten to fifteen people but the accused persons denied any of them being a part of that scuffle.

The police had recorded statements from the accused persons in the course of their investigation. During the hearing, the prosecution introduced most of these statements. Defence counsel objected to their introduction but the prosecuting officers stood their ground. Some of the defendants testified in Tamil. Interpreting for the Tamil-speaking witnesses turned out to be quite a task. The DPPs gave them a tough time, referring them to the statements they had made to the police, which statements differed from their evidence in court. The witnesses had a great deal of explanation to give and that meant much work for me.

I recall that I had a difficult time interpreting 'contradictions' in the police statements which the DPPs held some defendants had made in 'material particulars'. There are occasions when accused persons confronted with 'contradiction' will unhesitatingly say "that is not what I told the police. The interpreter then had misunderstood me and therefore the 'discrepancy'." The accused persons when cornered in court may blame it on the interpretation: "I never meant that ... the interpreter got me wrong ... the interpreter is wrong."

I must confess this 'allegation' against the interpreter (either during the recording of statements or in open court) was not used on me. The accused persons were gentlemenly in that respect – much to my relief. When the case was finally concluded and the verdict passed, I sighed with relief, having gone through one of my longest trials in the Subordinate Courts.

The Verdict

The trial judge, Roy Neighbour, ruled that he believed the testimony of the prosecution witnesses who saw the eight accused persons at the scene before and at the time the armed fight broke out. The judge said he was satisfied with the witnesses' identification of all the accused persons – he termed it 'good'.

The court held that the accused persons had taken the law into their own hands when they caused damage to Mohican's Pub and in attacking prosecution witness Mohan. The judge said that there was a common objective to cause hurt, as some of the accused persons clearly were armed with weapons and seen fighting at the scene.

Mr Neighbour therefore convicted all the eight accused persons of rioting with deadly weapons. Retnam Mohandas was further convicted of criminal intimidation and Anverdeen and Rajendran were convicted of disorderly behaviour. Sambalingam T and Natarajan both being above fifty years of age were spared the cane. The accused were sentenced as follows:

APPELLANT	CHARGE	SENTENCE IMPOSED
First appellant (Md Anverdeen Basheer Ahmad)	Rioting whilst armed with deadly weapon	36 months' imprisonment and six strokes of the cane
	Disorderly behaviour	Fined $500 with one week's imprisonment in default
Second appellant (Rupesh Kumar)	Rioting whilst armed with deadly weapon	36 months' imprisonment and six strokes of the cane
Third appellant (Rajendran s/o Rajagopal)	Rioting whilst armed with deadly weapon	36 months' imprisonment and six strokes of the cane
	Disorderly behaviour	Fined $500 with one week's imprisonment in default
Fourth appellant (Sambalingam T)	Rioting whilst armed with deadly weapon	36 months' imprisonment
Fifth appellant (Natarajan s/o Chinnaiah)	Rioting whilst armed with deadly weapon	36 months' imprisonment
Sixth appellant (Retnam Mohandas)	Rioting whilst armed with deadly weapon	Eight years' preventive detention and six strokes of the cane
	Criminal intimidation	
Seventh appellant (Sean Clinton)	Rioting whilst armed with deadly weapon	36 months' imprisonment and six strokes of the cane
Eighth appellant (Manogaran s/o Amirpan Ramaiah)	Rioting whilst armed with deadly weapon	36 months' imprisonment and six strokes of the cane

The Appeal

Six of the eight accused persons convicted by Judge Roy Neighbour appealed to the High Court. The appeal, heard by Chief Justice Yong Pung How in October 2004, was brought against both conviction and sentence.

The appellants were: Md Anverdeen (represented by Ramesh Tiwary), Rupesh Kumar and Sambalingam T (both represented by N Sreenivasan), Rajendran s/o Rajagopal (represented by Vasu and Gomez), Natarajan s/o Chinnaiah (represented by Thangavelu) and Retnam Mohandas (in person).

Yong Pung How CJ dealt with each appellant separately, first with their appeal against conviction, followed by the appeal against sentence. Having scrutinised the evidence of witnesses at the trial before the Subordinate Courts, the appeal judge dismissed all the appeals against conviction and sentence.

This case will remain in my memory for a long while. In all my years of service I had not interpreted in a trial as long as this – forty-two days. Neither had I been involved in a case with this number of accused persons and an equal number of prosecution witnesses choosing to testify in Tamil!

Somehow, it led to my recalling another case – more than thirty years ago, if my memory is still good – in the High Court before the late Justice Punch Coomaraswamy where eight or nine accused persons were charged with a capital offence. The prosecution later reduced the charge and the accused were accordingly convicted on a non-capital charge.

That case remains fresh in my mind because a young boy below sixteen years of age was jointly charged with the rest of the adults. When the capital charge was reduced and the adult accused were sentenced according to their respective roles in the commission of the offence, the underaged boy was placed on probation. For the first time I saw how a young mind could be manipulated by adult criminals to perform serious crime such as causing grievous bodily harm with deadly weapons whilst in their company.

Some years after dealing with that case, I happened to chance upon the boy at a gathering. The youth had become a responsible citizen, having completely turned over a new leaf. He walked up to me, introduced himself and briefly recalled our High Court encounter. He was then pursuing a course in a polytechnic. Once an incorrigible kid; now a humble caring adult!

He proudly spoke of his ambition and aspirations to prove to society that having been given a precious opportunity to change, he was resolved to show the law that paved the way for him that he would contribute and do his part for the betterment of society.

Hearing that, I was very proud of Singapore's justice system!

CASE 13

AN INTERESTING CASE THAT I FOLLOWED
Morbid jealousy

All this while I have shared cases that I have been involved in. In most cases I was glued to the interpreter's seat next to the accused throughout the trial, sometimes for days, sometimes for weeks. There have been cases where the interpretation work was less, perhaps only for the defence. The prosecution may have produced witnesses who did not require the service of interpreters.

There was this interesting case I followed very closely. By the time the case came up for hearing in the High Court, I had been transferred back to the Subordinate Courts. Recalling the good times I had in the High Court and the many thrills and excitement I had experienced interpreting in long capital cases, I followed this murder case – that of Krishnasamy Naidu who killed his wife outside her workplace.

The 18 May 2004 newspaper carried an article of a killing at Tuas. A 39-year-old Indian female had been hacked to death by her 43-year-old husband. Having read the report, I decided to closely follow the case especially when I learnt that the parties had frequented the Family Court next door.

The victim had obtained a PPO (Personal Protection Order) from a Family Court judge, for family violence on her by the accused, her husband. And just before her death, she had also applied for a DEO (a Domestic Exclusion Order – an order asking the court to exclude a person from home, due to violence). This application was pending at the time of the killing. The additional information had created anxiety and interest in me to want to follow the case – and I did. The killing is sad, unnecessary too, but I find the case interesting enough to share it with you!

The charge of murder read as follows: "You, G Krishnasamy Naidu, are charged that you on 17 May 2004, at about 6.20am, at Sony Display Device (Singapore), located at No 5 Tuas (Lane), Singapore, did commit murder by causing the death of one Chitrabathy d/o Narayanasamy, female, 39 years old, and you have thereby committed an offence punishable under section 302 of the Penal Code, Chapter 224."

The Trial

The accused (Krishnasamy) and the victim (Chitra) were husband and wife. They had married in June 1985 and had a son and a daughter.

Prosecution led evidence in the High Court hearing where the accused faced a murder charge that at about 6.20am of 17 May 2004, the accused had attacked the victim with a chopper at 5 Tuas Lane and killed her. The forensic pathologist for the case found two incised wounds on the victim's right arm, two incised wounds on her neck and two incised wounds on her back. The evidence also established that the accused intended to cause bodily injuries to the victim.

The accused relied on the defence of diminished responsibility. The defence alleged that the accused was suffering from Delusional Disorder Jealous-type which was a disease of the mind and that the disease had substantially impaired his mental responsibility for his acts in causing the victim's death. This disorder was referred to as "morbid jealousy" in the trial. The condition is sometimes referred to in the textbooks as "Othello Syndrome".

It was revealed in court that the victim had extra-marital affairs and those incidents had caused great anger, disappointment and frustration in the accused who went all out to trace his wife's infidelity.

In 1987, just after two years of her marriage to the accused, Chitra had an extra-marital affair with a Malaysian colleague at her workplace. She started going out with one Murugan, pretending to go to work. The accused looked for his wife at her workplace but was told that she was not at work. She returned home at around midnight. The accused questioned her as to her whereabouts suspecting that she was lying when she said she was at a friend's place at Block 5, Boon Lay.

The accused confronted and assaulted her. Chitra confessed that she was having an extra-marital affair with Murugan, who confessed to having had sex with Chitra at Strand Hotel. Advised by his mother to give Chitra a second chance, the accused decided not to divorce her. Perhaps at this point the couple ought to have first explored couple therapy to address the underlying marital issues.

In 1993, Chitra started work at Sony Display to supplement the family income. The accused was then working as a taxi driver. The two had a normal relationship until 2000.

In 2000, Chitra had an extra-marital affair with one Jayaseelan, an Indian national colleague at her workplace at Sony Display. This the accused came to find out by chance. Chitra had left home on the pretext of going to work the night shift but during this period of nine days, the factory was actually closed and all staff had to take leave. The accused called Chitra at about 9.30am and was told by an engineer who answered the call that the factory was closed. The accused therefore came to know that she had not gone to work. He questioned her on her whereabouts. She lied that she was at work at another plant. Infuriated by her string of lies, the accused hit her with a bamboo pole and caused a fracture of her right wrist. She made a police report and was hospitalised at National University Hospital (NUH) for four days.

The police visited Chitra when she was warded at NUH. She indicated to the police that it was a domestic dispute and did not wish to pursue the matter. The police gave the accused an oral warning that serious action would be taken against him if he repeated the offence.

The accused then discovered a telephone number from the Caller ID service. He called the number and through his investigative work, he found out that his wife was in a relationship with a Jayaseelan. After Chitra was discharged from NUH, the accused questioned her about Jayaseelan and assaulted her again. She bled from her face, mouth and nose. Chitra admitted she was having an affair with Jayaseelan. The accused got Chitra to call and invite Jayaseelan to the flat to talk. When Jayaseelan came over, both the accused and his brother-in-law Rajoo assaulted Jayaseelan who then admitted to having had sexual intercourse with Chitra on many occasions in Hotel 81.

Further suspecting that Chitra may be pregnant, the accused brought her to the Choa Chu Kang Polyclinic. There she was tested to be eight weeks' pregnant.

Back home the accused assaulted Chitra again. She confessed she was carrying Jayaseelan's baby. The accused paid $500 to a private clinic to have the baby aborted. He seriously considered divorcing Chitra. However, he forgave her for he loved her dearly. They got back to a good life.

Chitra then decided to divorce the accused. As a prelude she applied for a Personal Protection Order (PPO) against him in the Family Court. The accused threatened Chitra and demanded that she withdraw the PPO application to prevent her from seeking a divorce. But on 5 December 2001, the Family Court issued a PPO against the accused by consent. It is not known if there was a mandatory counselling order made as well!

In December 2001, the accused chanced upon Chitra's next affair – this time it was with an Indian national named Anan. But he did not monitor Chitra's movements; neither did he check her mobile phone. Anan worked at a flower shop near the accused's flat. Checking with StarHub through a cousin, the accused was able to confirm a SIM card registered in Chitra's name. When questioned later by the accused, Chitra admitted she had given the SIM card to Anan and confessed that she had gone to a hotel with him to have sexual intercourse on two occasions. The accused used a bamboo pole to beat Chitra.

On 10 January 2002, Chitra made a police report regarding the beating. In February 2002, Chitra informed the police she wanted to withdraw all the cases against the accused to keep the family together.

The accused was charged in court with three charges. The prosecution made an offer and the accused pleaded guilty to a reduced charge. He was sentenced to three months' imprisonment on 25 March 2002. When he was in prison, Chitra visited him regularly. On his release from prison, the accused went back to living with Chitra. Until February 2004, the accused had a normal relationship with Chitra.

Between 2003 and 2004, Chitra had another relationship – this time with one Michael Lee, a Malaysian who worked at the Sony plant at 1 Tuas Road. The two became lovers and would return home together after work. On some occasions they would kiss. On two occasions, once in 2003 and another in 2004, Chitra and Michael stayed at a chalet in East Coast Park with their children. They did so again on 19 and 20 January 2004. Michael touched Chitra's breasts and her private parts when she was sleeping.

From February 2004 onwards, Chitra began a relationship with Asokan s/o Muthu Suppiah aka Ashok who worked as a security guard at Sony Precision Engineering at 52 Tuas Ave 9. They had gotten to know one another in early February 2004 when travelling in the same vehicle after work. They soon exchanged mobile phone numbers and messages. Asokan invited Chitra to the Indian Association.

On 5 March 2004, on their second trip to the Indian Association, they held hands and kissed each other. On 26 March 2004, Chitra left home at 6.30pm claiming that she was going to a company barbecue party. The accused investigated and found out that Chitra's barbecue party was a total lie. He became angry that Chitra had lied to him. When she returned, the accused told her that he suspected she had returned from a pub and not a barbecue.

The accused asked Chitra to undress and he checked her panty to see if there was any evidence of semen. He then forcibly removed her bra and noticed love bites on her breasts. Whilst questioning her, the accused became angry. He had sexual intercourse with her, but she was unresponsive and reacted like a piece of wood.

The accused continued to check Chitra's mobile for numbers and messages and kept a close watch on her. He called for three or four 'family meetings' to clarify his suspicions.

On 7 April 2004, the accused fetched Chitra home from her workplace after her night shift. Angered by her remark that he was a madman, the accused picked up a knife from the kitchen and stabbed Chitra twice. His daughter had said that the accused, after stabbing Chitra, said Chitra would die and if she didn't, the accused would go to her workplace and kill her. On the same day the accused surrendered himself to the police.

On 10 April 2004, the accused was charged in court for stabbing his wife and was remanded for psychiatric assessment at the Institute of Mental Health (IMH). Almost every night at IMH, the accused had difficulty sleeping because he was thinking of Chitra and the children. On 7 May 2004, the accused was produced in court and released on bail. He was brought to the Family Court on the same day where a DEO was made against the accused, preventing him from entering the matrimonial flat.

The accused no longer harboured thoughts of killing Chitra. He still loved her very much. But he continued to feel that Chitra and Ashok were still intimate. He was proud of his twenty years of marriage and had tried to forgive Chitra despite her many affairs. The next few days, the accused constantly called Chitra's and Ashok's mobile phones and became very angry when both phones were switched off.

On 15 May 2004, the accused went to the temple to seek his God's guidance as to whether he should kill Chitra as he still loved her. He then thought of using a *parang* or chopper instead of a knife as she did not die the last time he stabbed her. He went to a hardware shop and asked for a *parang* but finally bought a chopper for $25.

On 17 May 2004, the accused arrived at 5 Tuas Lane. Inside the guard post he noticed a note on the board which prohibited his entry into the company's premises. The accused left the premises at about 6.00am as the company buses would soon be arriving. He retrieved the chopper from where he had hidden it.

The accused returned to the premises at 5 Tuas Lane and entered by climbing over the fence. He hid behind a meter room. At 6.25am, the accused saw Chitra walking into the factory. He approached her and handed her a piece of paper as if needing her signature on it. When she turned away from him, the accused suddenly took out his chopper and slashed her.

He left the scene and boarded a taxi for Toa Payoh. Along the way he called various people informing each one of them that he had killed Chitra.

The accused pleaded diminished responsibility in his defence. His lawyers relied on medical evidence substantially. The defence called two medical expert witnesses, both consultant psychiatrists. The accused had in April 2004 been admitted to IMH for the stabbing of his wife. The medical report stated that he had been well-behaved and co-operative. Not only did he give a clear account of what had happened, he also admitted he had been wrong in what he did.

After the killing of Chitra on 17 May 2004, the accused was charged with murder and remanded at Changi Prison Hospital for a psychiatric evaluation. Defence witness Dr Phang was of the opinion that the accused suffered from a delusional disorder, jealousy-type, which is a major form of mental illness characterised by the presence of non-bizarre delusions. It was clear the accused suffered an abnormal belief that his wife had been unfaithful.

The Verdict

Defence lawyers persuaded the trial judge to accept their argument that the accused suffered from morbid jealousy, citing instances of how each time Chitra had an extra-marital affair, the accused became infuriated and would beat her up, but each time he forgave her for he loved her very much.

The trial judge summed up thus: "On the totality of the evidence, I am not persuaded that the accused could have resisted his impulse to kill Chitra. That impulse stemmed from his obsession about her. He could not bear to divorce her or to let her be with other men.

"Such obsessive feelings are also found in persons who are extremely possessive and jealous, but not morbidly so. In my view, his feelings for her, however strong, did not substantially impair his mental responsibility for his actions leading to the killing of Chitra even though he was suffering from a mental disorder.

"The burden of proof is on the defence. I am afraid that the defence has failed to discharge its burden. I have to reject the defence of diminished responsibility and convict the accused on the charge of murder and sentence him according to the law."

The case of Krishnasamy took the Indian community by surprise. Although spousal infidelity is not uncommon, many who heard or read this case could not believe the life of Krishnasamy's wife, Chitra. Some felt she deserved the end that came upon her. Those who believed that one cannot take the law into one's hands thought Krishnasamy ought to have left it to the law to act.

In an era where divorce is so rampant, it is rather unbelievable there was a Krishnasamy who often contemplated divorcing Chitra but repeatedly forgave her for her infidelity, postponing his decision on a permanent separation with his wife! Perhaps Chitra had her personal reasons for drifting away from Krishnasamy each time she became attracted to a new man!

Counselling services for couples with matrimonial issues were available then. Perhaps Chitra was not aware of such services or did not approach any such agency for help. The unfortunate death could well have been avoided with the interception of appropriate help from a counselling agency!

CASE 14

A CASE THAT ATTRACTED INTERNATIONAL MEDIA
The riot that shook the nation

It was a Sunday, the 8th of December 2013. The evening was drawing to a close. After the weekend, it would be the start of another long work week!

As it has always been, the Tekka area in Little India, Singapore, on that Sunday was crowded with thousands of foreign workers, mainly Tamils, with Bangladeshis, Sri Lankans, Chinese nationals, Myanmarese, Indonesians, Filipinos and others from various countries beefing up Singapore's workforce.

There were the hundreds who met friends and countrymen from their homeland villages. Restaurants and eateries hired extra helping hands to cope with the large number of customers. Makeshift vegetable stalls along Buffalo Road and neighbouring lanes began clearing their produce to the last buyers for the day.

The air in the Tekka area was filled with a variety of languages – more noise than voices (the foreigners tended to speak loudly, raising their voices so that they could be heard amidst all the noise that 'polluted' the environment).

Nearby at Hampshire Road buses started to pile up, in readiness to pick up the foreign workers and return them to their different locations around the country. This was a special Sunday arrangement.

By about 8.30pm or so, these vehicles would leave the Tekka area filled with foreign workers who, having had a colourful, satisfying evening, were dashing back to their dormitories. For almost all of them, a new workweek would begin in the next few hours when they arrive at their bunks at the dormitories.

Shortly after 9.15pm, word went around that crowds of people had gathered at a spot where a fatal accident had taken place. At 9.27pm, a Cisco officer, Raymond Murugesu, called the Kampong Java Neighbourhood Police Centre (NPC) and lodged a report that a fatal accident had occurred along Race Course Road. He had been performing foreign worker management duties along that road. The officer also reported that a rowdy crowd had gathered at the incident scene.

On receiving the reports, the Rochor NPC, the Kampong Java NPC, the Traffic Police and the Singapore Civil Defence Force (SCDF) despatched officers to the scene of the incident.

What was the accident about and how serious was it?

Investigations revealed that on 8 December 2013, at about 8.30pm one Lee Kim Huat, aged 55 and employed as a bus driver by BT and Tan Pte Ltd to ferry foreign workers from Little India to their respective dormitories, had whilst moving off from the designated lot run over a 33-year-old foreign worker. The victim was Sakthivelu Kumaravelu, a construction worker with Heng Hup Soon Pte Ltd. The incident happened when the victim, drunk at the material time, was forcing his way into the bus.

Lee was making a left turn into Race Course Road when he realised he had run over an object. He later saw the victim pinned under the left rear wheel of the bus. Soon hundreds of foreign workers gathered around where Sakthivelu had been knocked down.

The crowd started shouting angrily, threatening to assault Lim and Wong, the timekeeper. By 9.30pm the police had arrived. The crowd had by then swelled to hundreds. They started throwing objects like stones, beer bottles, concrete slabs, rubbish bins and metal drain covers at the bus. Simultaneously, numerous '999' calls were made by members of the public to report the incident.

Police officers formed a cordon between the SCDF officers and the crowd. Several SCDF vehicles arrived at the scene to assist the extrication of the victim. These included an SCDF ambulance, QX454X. The crowd continued to behave violently towards the uniformed officers. The officers were pelted with stones, beer bottles and other projectiles.

Additional reinforcements were made. Resources from across various police land divisions were activated to quell the disturbance caused by the crowd and to restore order at the scene. As police rushed to the bus to assist with crowd control and to maintain law and order in the vicinity, the crowd began to cause extensive damage to the emergency response vehicles and private vehicles at the scene.

Soon Police Tactical Troops from the Special Operations Command (SOC) were activated. Announcements were made in English, Mandarin, Malay and Tamil via loudhailers, asking the crowd to disperse.

With their joint effort, the different police units brought the situation under control. Order was restored at about 11.45pm. Although the rioting left no death toll, several law enforcement officers were injured, and police and private vehicles damaged.

A total of twenty-four emergency vehicles were damaged. Five of these vehicles had been set on fire. Seven private vehicles were also damaged. Forty-three enforcement officers suffered injuries as a result of the incident.

The last time the Republic had witnessed a riot was in 1964. Strikes at workplace, mob violence on the streets, unlawful assembly and gathering of secret society groups had all been events of the past. Many read the newspapers in the days that followed the Little India riot with disbelief. Did all this happen at Tekka, they wondered. This most unexpected event should never occur again the government insisted. Almost every single Singaporean agreed.

The police patrolled the area where hours earlier violence, unrest and destruction of public property had prevailed. Their presence was to reassure Singaporeans that order and peace had been restored – that life was back to normal at Tekka, that people could move about in peace without any fear!

As a result of the riotous behaviour and extensive damage to property, arrests were made. After thorough screening and intensive investigation within its discretionary powers, the police decided to repatriate 53 persons picked up for interrogation.

Twenty-five of those arrested were produced in court and charged for various offences: unlawful assembly, destruction of property, setting an ambulance and police vehicles on fire, hurling objects and projectiles at police officers, refusing to comply with police request to disperse at the scene.

The Trial

All twenty-five accused persons were produced in Court 26. I assisted in reading out the charges to the respective accused persons. Pleas were then not recorded, that being a very first mention. A few of them were represented by lawyers but many were unsure what to do; some indicated that arrangements would soon be made for representation by lawyers.

Most of the accused persons were young. Some had not been working long in Singapore; several hadn't completed their period of contract at work. They looked lost and helpless. Many couldn't explain the reason for their involvement, apart from having joined fellow friends in whatever they did.

Here is a sample of one such charge preferred against one of the twenty-five accused persons:

"that you, on the 8th day of December 2013, at or about 10.50pm, in the vicinity of Race Course Road and Tekka Lane, Singapore, together with at least four other unknown subjects, were members of an unlawful assembly, whose common object was to commit an offence of mischief against a motorbus bearing registration number CB6978T, and in prosecution of the said common object of the assembly, you had used violence, namely (a) by throwing various objects at the said motorbus; (b) by kicking the said motorbus; (c) by throwing a partially burning object at the motorbus; and (d) by instigating other members of the unlawful assembly to attack the motorbus, and you have thereby committed an offence punishable under section 147 of the Penal Code. (Cap 224, 2008 Rev Ed)"

Although some accused persons had indicated they would challenge the charges against them, the State provided assistance to them by arranging pro bono services of lawyers who appeared on their behalf, mitigated and made appropriate representations for reduction of severity of the charges.

Most Indians were deeply appreciative of the fact that the State considered all the circumstances of the case against each accused and charged the accused with offences that befitted their respective conduct, Some accused were hence spared the cane. The sentences imposed by judges were commensurate with the offences. Some felt however that the State should have pressed for harsher, longer terms of imprisonment!

Investigations into the events that night revealed that the Tekka area and in particular the 'kodai canteen' behind Buffalo Road, were used predominantly by foreign workers. They gathered there during weekends to meet up with friends and relatives (mostly from their home town in South India) not only to catch up on the latest news, but also for long drinking sessions.

Evidence was led indicative of the fact that drinking alcohol was one of the main issues. The investigation also found that the behaviour – rowdyism, pelting police officers with projectiles, injuring police and public officers, causing extensive damage to police and other vehicles, refusing to disperse when called upon by the police – of the hundreds of workers at the scene of the incident related to alcoholism.

A Committee of Inquiry (COI) was specially convened in February 2014. Mr G Pannir Selvam was appointed chairman of the COI.

The COI spoke to many foreign workers, including twenty foreign workers who were to be repatriated for their involvement in the riot. It visited the site of the riot, the dormitories and quarters where the foreign workers resided, and areas where these workers regularly congregated. The COI also invited members of the public to submit accounts of the incident.

Since the inquiry drew a great amount of attraction from Singaporeans at large and the media – both local and foreign –

the State Courts gathered an experienced team of support staff during the proceedings.

Not all reports on the Little India riot were accurate. International media such as the *Sun TV* from Tamil Nadu did not hesitate to imply that the riot erupted as a result of racial conflict, claiming that Indian nationals residing in Singapore were attacked in Singapore, resulting in violence and chaos. The *Sun TV* blatantly reported that an Indian worker was deliberately pushed out of a bus and killed, resulting in a protest by fellow workers that escalated into riots. The news further said that Chinese came to the area and attacked the foreign Tamilians. The inaccuracies in the report were pointed out to *Sun TV*. The agency apologised and aired a corrected version of the report.

Many of the foreign workers were predominantly Tamil-speaking. I was assigned along with my colleague Sakthi, a senior interpreter, to handle the number of Tamil-speaking witnesses. Although the inquiry dragged on for a total of twenty-four hearing days and the sessions with some of the Tamil witnesses were lengthy and tiring, Sakthi and I shared the workload and discharged our duties professionally.

I had previously worked with the COI chairman, Mr Selvam, in the High Court during my early days when he was a High Court judge. I had always found it interesting interpreting in Mr Selvam's court. Having spent many interview sessions with Tamil-speaking foreign workers in preparation for the inquiry, Mr Selvam was well fortified with sufficient material to examine witnesses.

He held talks with a number of foreign workers who had been detained for their involvement in the riot. Mr Selvam was accompanied to the prisons by a very senior interpreter, Suseela, who assisted him in interviewing them to obtain as much information as possible on what the foreign workers had witnessed at the scene and the role some of them had played during the riot.

Most of the foreign workers who took the stand at the inquiry were from Tamil Nadu, South India. They had come from different villages. Mr Selvam, being thoroughly familiar with the area and villages mentioned, was able to engage the witnesses in conversation, livening up the hearing. Apart from posing questions, he made a pertinent joke or two in between the examination which helped draw answers from the otherwise tense witnesses, some of whom were fearful that a repatriation home to India was unavoidable.

The COI conducted its public hearing in open court, between 19 February 2014 and 26 March 2014. The statements of 323 witnesses were reviewed. The committee heard the oral evidence of 93 such witnesses in all. The COI also viewed footage of the bus accident and riot. After the public hearing, the committee interviewed two foreign workers who had been convicted and sentenced for rioting.

All 53 foreign workers who were to be repatriated in December 2013 for their involvement in the event were invited by the COI to be interviewed on a voluntary basis before they departed Singapore. Twenty agreed to do so. These workers spoke to the COI on 18 December 2013 and 20 December 2013 respectively. Nineteen of them were from Tamil Nadu in India and one was from Bangladesh.

The COI completed and submitted its report on 27 June 2014. One of its recommendations was to curb the sale of alcoholic drink, thereby containing the influence of liquor on drinkers.

This was my first experience interpreting in an inquiry of this nature. It had attracted the interest of various races in Singapore as well as a large presence of media, both local and foreign. It was quite intimidating as I had to be aware that I was being 'watched' throughout the inquiry, but working with known faces in the committee made it less stressful.

MY JOURNEY THROUGH THE JUDICIARY

I joined the then District and Magistrate's Courts as a student interpreter in September 1967 and have spent fifty-two years in the Judiciary – twenty years in the High Court and the remaining years in the Subordinate Courts (now the State Courts). Although I was trained to interpret in a variety of cases, criminal trials remained my love. Reading grounds of decisions by judges has been my favourite pastime.

Throughout the years I have witnessed many different cases featuring various sets of facts. They have appeared in different forms: criminal, civil and family.

Each case was a fresh experience and a new lesson. In the early years, the life of an interpreter was less settled. The courts were situated in different areas: the Criminal Courts at South Bridge Road, the Civil Courts at Empress Place, the Traffic Courts at Sepoy Lines, the Coroner's Court at Outram Road and the Syariah Court at Fort Canning. Travelling between the courts was itself an experience as much as the nature of the cases!

A recollection of the lower courts

I walked into the old lower courts, initially named the Police Courts, then renamed the District and Magistrate's Courts, as a student interpreter some time in 1967. How did I find the old building, situated at South Bridge Road, then? What was

I met with senior officers at HR for the transfer. A young officer introduced herself to me and arranged to accompany me to my new place of work at Paterson Road. The officer, whose name I now don't recall, was very encouraging. She sounded impressed with my experience in service and the fact that I had by then served twenty years in the High Court.

Our cab drove to the Orchard Road area, which I had always never been familiar with, and up a slope into a lane that appeared to have lots of trees and greenery. It passed two international schools, a canteen, and finally stopped at an old building that looked like a school. I recognised it as the old Teachers' Training College, a three-storey building which had served as a college for trainee teachers.

Walking into the building, I was referred to the Registrar, a young judicial officer totally unfamiliar to me. The welcome the Registrar gave me was as if I was reporting as a freshman. I was shown around the small building comprising a few courtrooms which were previously classrooms, a registry managed by a handful of officers, and a crammed room with lots of files spilling over.

The orientation session was over in less than an hour. I then met up with my work team, Gowri and Santha. It was a pleasure to meet both of them; they were close friends of mine although we had never worked together. They were equally glad to meet me and to have to work with me. Gowri, particularly, was well acquainted with me; we had first met at the interview as candidates for the job. She was a capable young lady who could be trusted with responsibility. Both ladies realised how much I missed my High Court life and endeavoured to keep me occupied. My transfer was so abrupt that I had reported at Paterson without even taking my drinking glass or mug along.

Gowri offered me a new mug and showed me around the cute, small pantry the staff had been furnished with.

The next two days were spent walking around the courts observing my two mentors as they introduced me to work processes at the Family Court. It was my first time meeting with the Family Court judges. I had to introduce myself to the judicial officer on duty when I took parties before her on my maiden venture. The young female judicial officer looked at me suspiciously as I gave an account of myself, including how I had been transferred from the High Court.

Soon I got to meet the rest of my colleagues and work with them at different times. Work at the Family Court was interesting.

My role as a court mediator

Most interesting at the Family Court was our mediation role as interpreters. We mediated not only in maintenance issues between warring spouses but also between family members seeking Personal Protection (Court) Orders for violence.

Parties quarrelling over maintenance often got carried away by emotional issues between them. Resolving the issues sometimes became pretty difficult as the parties refused to compromise, especially when there was an intention to proceed with divorce action at a later stage. When divorce is in the mind of either one or both parties, mediation over maintenance becomes extremely difficult. Sometimes parties remain stubborn over small sums, refusing to come to terms. In the end, it is the children of the marriage who are the victims.

Justice will not be done if I fail to mention the role of the Family Court judges. There was just a handful of them. Most were not much experienced but each of them was brilliant, consistent and very down-to-earth in their own ways. They exhibited patience and tolerance in handling parties appearing before them, many electrified with emotions and dampened with sorrow and frustration.

There were more female judges than male, and most male litigants were unhappy to see their greater number. Some commented that female judges decided cases in favour of female parties, though this was entirely without basis. Some even openly remarked that the Women's Charter protected the women and that it worked to the detriment of men.

Divorce in the Family Courts

In April 1997 it was decided that all divorce matters would be heard by judges of the Family Court, the jurisdiction to hear family-related cases being transferred to the judges of the Subordinate Courts. In line with the decision, a judge with whom I had worked in the High Court was transferred to the Family Court. He was to hear uncontested divorce matters.

Mr Tan Puay Boon reported at the Family Court and immediately got into action. Mr Tan had always been looked up to and admired for his good nature and his cool, calm and accommodative personality. Almost all the staff loved to work alongside the down-to-earth Mr Tan. It was a pleasure doing mediation in maintenance cases with him. The staff did not mind working late with him during night court sessions even if it meant going past 8pm. Never before had there ever been a judicial officer who respectfully referred to an interpreter as "my colleague".

The Family Court at Paterson was kept busy with a huge number of cases. It was a marvel that a three-storey building as small as the Family Court could deal with cases in such large numbers. We felt crammed most of the time, space constraint being our frequent complaint. But hardly anything could be done about that. Staff at Paterson continued to work diligently giving their best at all times, their contribution deeply appreciated by the judicial officers.

The building was 'temporary' or at least it had been so for almost the previous ten years. A new Family Court at Havelock was expected to be ready in early 2002. So life went on with the hustle and bustle of non-stop activity. Human traffic flowed throughout the morning, afternoon and even the evening with the presence of litigants and their supporters during the night court sessions.

Senior officers from the Subordinate Courts did come by to either visit or inspect the Family Court. They may have appreciated the service rendered by Family Court staff but it is a pity that such sentiments were never shared with the staff.

Courts in the woods
Fortunately our pleasant environment made up for all that. It was always green and fresh with trees and branches, leaves and flowers. The occasional appearance of pretty squirrels added colour to the enchanting environment. Watching children from the neighbouring Australian and Canadian schools doing physical workouts in the field was a refreshing change after a long session with quarrelling parties bickering over dollars and cents.

Food was difficult to come by in the courts situated in the woods of Paterson but staff either took lunch-time walks to the nearby Wisma Atria/Orchard area where there were plentiful stalls and shops, or bought and stocked up food weekly.

In early 2002 it was officially announced that the courts at Paterson would, in the next three months or so, move to the newly renovated Family Court building (formerly the Labour Court building) at Havelock Square. So it was serious packing of everything at Paterson in the midst of our daily duties during the next three months.

The Family Court at Paterson had been set up way back in 1993. Colleagues who had worked there since its inception felt they would miss the pleasant environment of the woods. For many it was hardly a welcome move. In my case, it had been a mere six years at Paterson since being transferred out of the High Court. I had in those years acclimatised myself to the work and the location. The very thought of having to move again was annoying and cumbersome. But move I must if I chose to remain working.

Counsellors of the Family Court and me.

New premises at Havelock Square

By April 2002 the Family Court was all set to begin operation at Havelock Square. Renovation to the then existing building was massive. Provision had been made for rooms to hold mediation and counselling sessions, together with space for meetings and training sessions. To maintain continuity of work, the Head Interpreters decided to leave the last batch of interpreters at Paterson to operate the new courts at Havelock.

With more space and larger courtrooms work appeared less cumbersome even though the volume of work never changed. I was immersed in unending work related to divorces, ancillary issues, maintenance disputes and violence amongst family members leading to applications for Personal Protection Orders (PPO).

Soon, I heard rumours that the administration would recall me to the main office to take on a Deputy Head role. By then I was quite settled with Family Court matters and I was keen to stay put there.

I had a heart-to-heart talk with my head, Ajmer Singh, who had known me for many years. Ajmer valued my long service, especially in the High Court, and had been concerned about me. He was of the opinion that one of the reasons for my transfer to the Subordinate Courts was to be duly considered for promotion to Head Interpreter. He spoke openly about me getting promoted, a stage that had eluded me more than once. I had missed such an opportunity before I left the High Court and he was aware of that. As rumoured, it happened. I was recalled to the main office as Deputy Head. In my place another senior officer was appointed to lead the team at the Family Court.

The Community Court

Youths who were past sixteen years of age and could not be tried in the Juvenile Court were tried in the adult court. In 1985, an amendment to the law was introduced to give a second chance to youthful offenders.

The Community Court, to try these youthful offenders who were between sixteen and eighteen years of age, was opened on 29 May 2008. To inform the public about the Community Court, the media arranged interviews with serving officers in the Subordinate Courts. As part of the arrangement, *Vasantham* interviewed me for the Tamil news. The two-minute interview was aired on 29 May 2008 during the news.

Mr Bala Reddy, formerly from the Attorney-General's Chambers, and who was serving as Principal District Judge, was transferred to the Community Court to sit as District Judge to hear these cases. Mr Reddy had some months earlier requested that I work with him in the said court and, for the next three years, I served as Interpreter of the Community Court under Mr Reddy.

Many youths in that age group appeared before Judge Reddy. They were tried mainly for violence, molest, outraging modesty, unlawful assembly and rioting.

Mr Reddy proved real stern with the youthful offenders sometimes sending them home to change into their school attire, remove some conspicuous tattoo or go for a haircut before appearing before him in open court.

I saw that most parents of these youths often claimed that their sons were innocent, blaming other youths for influencing their sons and leading them to commit the offence. Many such youths were referred to court counsellors who interviewed them and prepared reports to assist the judge in delivering appropriate sentences.

The counsellors worked hand in hand with Judge Reddy and spent many hours deliberating on reports prepared. One Viven Kwek and a Japanese gentleman whose name I recall as Joseph Ozawa were such lovely officers to work with. They were both committed to their work and sacrificed many hours of their personal time. Together we served the best we could, relying on each other's experience and expertise.

Concerned about the number of Indian youths convicted in the Community Court, Mr Reddy was keen to liaise with groups engaged in community service. Mr Reddy felt some of our cases could be referred or reassigned to a body or institution that dealt with such referrals and he assigned volunteers to follow up on the cases referred by our in-house counsellors.

Efforts were made to touch base with organisations that could be counted on. Mr Reddy and I met up with officials of the Hindu Endowments Board. Separately I met officials of the Hindu Centre and SINDA. The response from these organisations was encouraging.

Head of Indian Interpreters

In late 2009 there was a need to appoint a new head of Indian interpreters because the Punjabi head, Lashman Singh, was due to retire having reached the compulsory age of retirement. There was no doubt this time that it was going to be a Tamil interpreter, there being no other senior Punjabi officer in service.

As I was approaching my sixtieth birthday, Management was slightly hesitant to give me the opportunity. After some consideration, Senior District Judge Tan Siong Thye called me in to his chambers, and informed me that I was to head the Indian Interpreters. I had been acting Head at the time.

I remained the Head for two full years before I retired at 62 years of age. Working under Mr Tan was demanding. He meant business and worked tirelessly past the official working hours. Kind and concerned as he was towards his staff, he never hesitated to draw maximum contribution from them.

Doing administrative work and attending meetings and briefings were new to me. I struggled because of my lack of computer knowledge. Meeting deadlines for correspondences and reports was quite a challenge. I badly needed assistance. Three kind staff members, Gowri, Suseela and Anita, were at hand when work took the toll on me. Life as the head wouldn't have been so interesting if not for the trio who assisted me in every way.

DPP Lau Wing Yam (in the foreground) in the Interpreters' room.

With Zakaria Imal on my right and Daniel Ang on my left.

During the two years, I also enjoyed working with colleagues Daniel and Zakaria, the heads of the Chinese and Malay sections. We spent many hours at and off work, sharing staff problems, managing stressful assignments handed us and discussing common issues faced by heads. That we cooperated to the best of our ability and achieved the best for the department was something we were very proud of.

In September 2010 I stepped down as Head and was succeeded by a female officer who became the first female Head of the Indian Interpreters' section.

Life on Extended Service

The courts organised a farewell lunch for six officers including me to express its gratitude for our long service. At the lunch I was presented with a gift and a valedictory letter signed by then president, Mr S R Nathan.

Retirement lunch on 19 January 2011.

Mr Tan Siong Thye requested that I consider working on an extended service after my retirement. He felt I could still contribute for the betterment of the courts. I thought about his proposal and returned to work on 20 September as a re-employed retiree.

For the next three years I was back in the courtrooms reading charges and statements of facts and mitigating. In between I did trials which went on for two, three or more days. These included civil and criminal trials. After the third year I developed health issues and found it an agony interpreting trials for long hours.

The trial judges were understanding when I explained my medical problem. They were prepared to bear with my need for frequent toilet breaks. As Judge Roy Neighbour put it, "as we age we must take good care of our health". Although the judges were considerate of my situation, I began to feel uncomfortable sharing my health problem with female judicial officers.

Unable to cope with long trials I decided in mid-2014 that I should stop work. I met the Registrar Ms Jennifer Marie in her chambers one afternoon and shared my feelings. She felt if it was the nature of the work that was troubling me, I should reconsider my decision to leave. Ms Marie said I could continue to contribute my services with a change of job. She said I could help out in a new Division to be set up for operation on 1 November 2014. Mr Bala Reddy was to head the new division which would handle issues related to the Protection from Harassment Act (POHA). She suggested I meet up with him.

Mr Reddy had months earlier mentioned his return to the State Courts in July when the new division was to be introduced and he had invited me to work with him. Soon, I requested to move to the new division.

Transfer to Community Justice and Tribunals Division (CJTD)

In November 2014 the Community Justice and Tribunals Division (CJTD) came into effect. It started as a small division handling harassment complaints (POHA) and the Small Claims Tribunal. I was transferred from the Interpreters' section to the new division which operated temporarily from the Crime Registry. I had by then been in the Interpreters' section for almost forty-eight years.

I had known Mr Bala Reddy during my High Court days when Mr Reddy served as State Counsel in the Attorney-General's Chambers. I had also worked with Mr Reddy between 2006 and 2018 when Judge Reddy sat in the Community Court. And so in November 2014, I was privileged to work under him again in the newly established Community Justice and Tribunals Division (CJTD).

The official CJTD office was ready by April 2015 and the entire division moved into the newly established premises with the Chief Justice officially opening it on 24 April 2015.

My role in handling POHA matters was that of an assessor/consultant. The work included seeing parties, taking down complaints and assessing the risk factors involved, guiding applicants rather than advising them what to do. Most applicants spoke English and there was very little interpreting as such. I thoroughly enjoyed my role as consultant. I had always enjoyed this part of my working life. I last was involved in similar work at the Family Court at Paterson where I assisted in resolving issues between spouses and conflicting family members. My experience and age were important factors in the execution of my duties as a consultant.

In October 2015 the government introduced the Community Disputes Resolution Tribunals (CDRT) to hear neighbour disputes. Soon the workload increased. Today, CJTD is a large work force, also overseeing Small Claims cases and Employment Claims Tribunal cases from 1 April 2017, the division has grown much larger in size and volume.

How well an officer discharges his or her duty depends very much on how he or she is moulded, guided and nutured. Principal District Judge Reddy is a highly talented, versatile officer with more than thirty-five years of experience in the different fields of the legal fraternity.

By nature a strict and demanding but well-meaning officer, Mr Reddy has faith and trust in his colleagues and fellow workers. This explains why CJTD is able to clear its workload steadily and thus develop a happy work environment.

What is peculiar about CJTD is that the division employs fairly elderly workers. In the words of Mr Reddy, "CJTD is an elderly-friendly" division!

The CJTD team – a big happy family.

A Day in Court

The State Courts in Singapore has in the last three years successfully organised a programme called 'A Day in Court'. In this whole-day programme, a group of students are invited to sit in and watch the actual functioning of the court. The students are taken on a tour of the different sections of the State Courts and briefed by judicial officers on different aspects of the courts' functions. The students later role-play as court officers, prosecutor, and defence counsel in a mock court session.

In its third year, I was requested to take on a role in the mock session. Although I had not attended or participated in either of the two previous sessions, I accepted to play a role this time, with enthusiasm and keen interest. Set against a background of a 19-year-old charged with unlawful assembly, with a pre-sentencing report favouring the youthful offender a chance to be placed on probation, I played a judge delivering the sentence.

The students, coached and mentored diligently by colleagues of mine, performed beyond expectation. It was a good experience not only for the teenage students but for court administrators as well. The teachers who accompanied their students were just as enthusiastic when they watched them perform the roles. Some complimented the State Courts for taking great pain to organise such a useful, informative session.

It was a pleasure, and a memorable experience, working alongside young students, prospective professionals and the future leaders of this country.

Talking about CJTD, I must not fail 7to touch on the Student Representative Programme initiated by the State Courts. This programme, introduced in June 2016, allows law undergrads to serve in the CJTD. The students play an important role, assisting applicants at CJTD who are non-conversant in English and unable to fill in application forms and write affidavits.

This special programme not only provides crucial service to the public but gives the law undergrads an opportunity to gain experience whilst volunteering. They sit with the consultants occasionally to observe and learn the different processes at CJTD as well as enjoy first-hand experience dealing with the variety of complainants that come before the consultants.

Criminal Law Advisory (CLAC) review sessions

The CLAC reviews and examines the evidence in every case where a suspected criminal is detained under the Criminal Law (Temporary Provisions) Act (Singapore) (CLTPA). The CLAC then makes recommendations to the President to cancel, confirm or vary the orders issued.

This Singapore statute allows the executive branch of the government of Singapore to order that suspected criminals be detained without trial. Introduced in 1955, the validity of the Act was most recently extended in November 2013, and it will remain in force till 20 October 2019.

The Act is only used as a last resort when a serious crime has been committed and a court prosecution is not possible because witnesses are unwilling or afraid in cases related to secret societies, drug trafficking and loansharking.

Mr Lee Kuan Yew, Singapore's first Prime Minister, had supported the law. He once said, *"Let us face the facts: either we bring these gangsters to trial, or we do nothing, or we lock them up without trial. Well, we prefer to bring them to trial if we could. As I know, and I think every practising lawyer in town knows, the point is now reached when police officers frankly admit that gangsters are not scared of the police anymore ... Now quite frankly, either you surrender and say, well the judicial process is inadequate and therefore we have been beaten by gangsters, or we say, well what do we do about it? I say, if there is no other way, then we had better deal with them firmly."*

Cases are referred to the CLAC for review (hearing) after a Detention Order or Police Supervision Order has been issued by the Minister.

I have over the many years as an interpreter assisted in such review sessions.

The detainee or police supervisee will be informed of the grounds for his detention or police supervision, and be given the right to make his own representations to the Committee.

He may also be represented by a lawyer of his choice. The CLAC, comprising prominent private citizens, will sit to scrutinise the evidence and may examine the detainee or police supervisee, investigating officers and witnesses on the grounds of the case.

After a Detention Order has been made or after its expiry, the Minister may direct that the person be subject to police supervision for a period not exceeding three years. Supervision orders must also be referred to the CLAC and reviewed by the President.

Detainees under the Criminal Law (Temporary Provisions) Act are allowed to appeal to the Home Minister for an early release. This the detainee can do by making representations to the CLAC. These are committees formed by the Minister, each committee consisting of no fewer than two persons.

The panel will consist of three persons (on occasions, two): a chairman, assisted by two others. Members of the panel are most often practising lawyers who volunteer their good services to assist the Minister in reviewing detainees' cases.

Detainees often appear in person to present their appeals. Families of some detainees engage lawyers to represent them. But these are few in number. In the early years, detainees often spoke in Tamil, or at least requested the services of an interpreter. Those days the detainees were older.

Despite the long list of antecedents and incidents spelt out in the charges against the detainees, I had always felt that youthful offenders ought to be given a second chance, i.e. at least the possibility of an early release be strongly considered.

My observation is that these detainees in gangster-related activities since their teenage days, often work under peer pressure! Where there is no representation by a lawyer, there is this onerous task on the interpreter to listen carefully and 'represent' the detainee by presenting his appeal with thorough clarity.

Often the youthful offender will deny the incidents in the charges. Where the detainee is unable to absolve himself from accusations spelt out, the detainee will attempt to mitigate his position, apologising for his involvement. Some detainees who have pursued studies at the time of detention will seek the Committee's assistance for an early release to continue their studies. Cases of early marriage, some with unmarried partners expecting babies, are also cited as ground for sympathetic consideration.

I have always been keen to get involved in such review sessions – assisting in the interpretation, and understanding the plight of a young person who has indulged himself in criminal/unlawful activities. It has been a few years since I last interpreted in a review session. I miss all those good old days!

Appearance on hoarding

In January 2017, the State Courts decided to publicise the technological advancements it was introducing in the various court processes. In this regard arrangements were made to feature some officers on the hoardings that led from Chinatown MRT station to the entrance of the court building.

The hoarding featuring me along the passageway leading from the court building to the Chinatown MRT station.

A date was set for about twelve staff members to be photographed by a set of professional photographers. The crew of cameramen and designers took us through a lengthy session, coaching us on various poses. In March 2017, when I returned from a holiday, I was told that some of the photos were on the hoarding leading to the entrance of the State Courts.

To my surprise there was a full-length photo of me. Many asked why I was gesticulating in the photo. I was teased about it. Some said my stretching out both hands showed that I had finally given up on work and myself. One meaningful suggestion was that I was rewarded by State Courts for my fifty years of dedication in the Civil Service, having served only the Judiciary throughout.

Oral History interview
Some time in early 2017, I was invited for an interview for the Department's Oral History preservation. I remember mentioning the various transformations in public service that were initiated by the Subordinate Courts/State Courts in the last decade:

1. The Bail Centre: Bail processing which sometimes took one day was shortened to fifteen minutes
2. The Bail Centre at Court 26 was moved to the Crime Registry
3. Saturday Court 26: Bail officers were stationed at Court 26
4. Night courts started operation in 1991
5. The night courts which operated as 13N/14N on the third floor were moved to Court 26N/Court

25N on the ground floor, for the convenience of the public

6. Manual System (Records) were computerised: Ticks (the processing of traffic charges between the police and the courts), Scrims I, Scrims II (the registration and management of criminal cases)
7. Civil litigation moved from manual filing to EFS to e-litigation/CJTS
8. Video conference using a Galaxy tablet for remote court proceedings (e.g. reading charges to persons in hospital)
9. Introduction of iPads to read charges in courts
10. Court 26 heard DAC (District Arrest Cases) and MAC (Magistrate's Arrest Cases) in 1995 and subsequently Court 23 became operative doing MAC cases
11. Maintenance Mediation Centre (MMC) was set up in the Family Court in 2007
12. Some officers appointed to serve as Concierges
13. The courts library was moved up to the seventh floor, from the ground floor
14. Number of courtrooms increased from 26 to 40
15. Security clearance when entering the State Courts building was introduced
16. A large canteen existed on the ground floor of the Subordinate Courts and was later removed
17. A fully covered walkway from the MRT station to the courts building was erected

Public Service (PS) 21 Award

The Public Service honours its dedicated officers every year by awarding officers who had gone the extra mile in serving the public. One morning whilst reading my emails at 8.30am, I was surprised to receive a mail from my department with an announcement that I was to receive the PS21 award.

Totally taken by surprise, I shared it with Mr Reddy, my Principal District Judge. He pointed out that the award was a prestigious one given to an officer in recognition of his contribution to the country through the Civil Service. He further shared that I ought to be proud to receive the PS21 award especially because the State Courts had recommended to the Public Service that I be given the said award.

Judge also pointed out that in September 2017, I would be completing fifty years in the Civil Service, having served the Judiciary and that the award presentation came at just the right time.

I attended the award presentation ceremony on 29 May 2016 at Gardens by the Bay, accompanied by my wife who has been a pillar of strength in my life since our marriage in 1973. The Awards were presented by Mr Teo Chee Hean, Deputy Prime Minister and Mr Peter Ho, Head, Civil Service. There was a large pool of recipients and the two-and-a half-hour ceremony was very well organised. It ended with a sumptuous dinner.

In conjunction with the award presentation ceremony there was a meeting with the President of the Republic for all award recipients at the Istana. I had never been to the Istana grounds before. As such I was overly excited and very much looked forward to it. It rained the whole afternoon but nothing deterred the proud recipients from making their way to the Istana grounds.

The organisers were on hand with huge umbrellas to assist the recipients board the arranged buses which transported us to the hall where the reception had been scheduled. The two-hour programme was carried out swiftly and crisply.

President Tony Tan met all recipients in six groups as he walked through the ballroom. We had been briefed earlier that recipients were expected to create topics for conversation with the President as he approached each group. When the President met my group, I spoke of the experience I had working with Mr Tan when he was a Member of Parliament in the 1980s.

I recalled Mr Tan visiting Telok Blangah constituency during a General Election week when he popped in to meet party cadres and supporters at work assisting the Member of Parliament of Telok Blangah constituency. He had sat in with volunteers to have a brief tea session. Mr Tan could not recall the details of the visit but remembered such a visit.

The President said I appeared to be a senior officer in the Civil Service and enquired about my job and the history. When

Photo of me receiving my PS21 award, and the souvenir trophy.

told that I was from the Judiciary and that in September 2017 7I would be completing fifty years in the Singapore Civil Service, he gave a wide smile, patted me on my back and commented, "Amazing."

When I brought the prestigious PS 21 award to show Mr Bala Reddy and Ms Jennifer Marie in the office two days later, I spoke with enthusiasm of my feelings and emotion whilst at the two ceremonies and how honoured I felt receiving an award having served the Civil Service close to fifty years.

I told Ms Marie how extremely proud I was when the National Anthem was sung at the Istana, although I had on numerous occasions in my life stood proud when the anthem was played.

REFLECTIONS

In September 2017, I completed fifty years in the Civil Service, having served all those years in the Judiciary – the Subordinate Courts (State Courts) and in the High Court.

Perhaps I should console myself that I had over the long period of time at work played a small but significant role as an officer of the court. My contract expired in March 2019. Friends felt I could continue for another few years. But I felt otherwise. I did feel upset at the very thought of leaving the job, workplace and the people I had been associated with. Some colleagues have over the years become friends, some close and dear. I sure would miss them. But leave I had to.

Because of my love for work and the life in the courts, I have devoted the greater part of my life to work. My family, especially my four grandchildren aged four, six, ten and thirteen, have not spent much time with me.

The two boys have grown; the girls are growing up fast. Besides spending more time with them, I also need to put aside time for my personal interests such as reading, writing (in Tamil and English), listening to songs from old movies (I have a long list!) some of them as old as seventy years and volunteering my service to the temples which I have loved doing for many years.

After fifty-two years of working life I now have the opportunity to stay cool with what I love to do!

Judges and court administrators as I saw them

Judicial officers generally don't interact closely with interpreters – at least not as closely as they do with other court administrators. There are rare occasions of 'closeness' when an interpreter gets to do long hearing cases. When this happens, the interpreter serves as an officer of the court, and is more than a mere mouthpiece.

How was the relationship with my colleagues and judicial officers?

Working closely with judges during trials, interpreters get to understand their judges better and see the caring side of judicial officers. I particularly witnessed and appreciated some such judges after my compulsory retirement at sixty-two years of age, when my health deteriorated.

During my twenty years (1976–1995) at the High Court, I acquired a wealth of experience and knowledge from working with the following judges:

Justice Wee Chong Jin, Justice F A Chua, Justice T Kulasekaram, Justice Choor Singh, Justice T S Sinnathuray, Justice L P Thean, Justice Punch Coomaraswamy, Justice A V Winslow, Justice Denis D'Cotta, Justice Lai Kew Chai, Justice Chan Sek Keong, Justice Chao Hick Tin, Justice Yong Pung How, Justice M Karthigesu, Justice S Rajendran, Justice Goh Joon Seng and Justice G P Selvam.

Some events of note in that period were:

- Chan Sek Keong was the first person to be appointed a Judicial Commissioner on 1 July 1986. He served as Attorney-General between 1 May 1992 and 10 April 2006 before he was appointed as Chief Justice on 11 April 2006. In August 2008

he became the first Singaporean and local law graduate to become an honorary bencher of Lincoln's Inn.
- Chan Seng Onn was appointed Solicitor-General on 1 June 2001.
- The first female High Court Judge, Lai Siu Chiu, was appointed on 2 May 1994.
- Lee Seiu Kin, who served as a Judicial Commissioner between 15 October 1997 and 14 October 2002, served as Second Solicitor-General between 15 October 2002 and 10 April 2007, and was appointed a Judge with effect from 11 April 2007.
- Wee Chong Jin was Singapore's first Asian Chief Justice and, having been appointed at the age of forty-five years, also the youngest. In addition, having held the post for over twenty-seven years, he was the longest-serving Chief Justice in Singapore and in a Commonwealth country.

More than thirty years of my career in the Judiciary were spent in the Subordinate Courts/State Courts.

I take this opportunity to mention a few judicial officers whose humanitarianism touched me, especially when I struggled with Tamil-speaking witnesses in lengthy trials: DJ Siva Shanmugam, DJ Jasvender Kaur, former DJ Roy Neighbour and former DJ Low Wee Ping both when he was Registrar of High Court and Registrar of Subordinate Courts.

When writing about myself, the experiences I have gathered, I wish to highlight some events which I feel are worthy of mention.

Judge Bala Reddy

A case of theft came before the Community Court. A 19-year-old youth was charged with petty theft. A probation report was called for. His counsellor Viven spent some time with the youth's parents to collect information on the youth, his behaviour, his attitudes, his habits and circle of friends.

The parents of the youth, the only child in the family, were interviewed. My services were required as I sat in with Viven when she spent a good part of a Saturday morning interviewing the youth's mother. The middle-aged lady was quite willing to share information on the family of three.

It was clear throughout the interview that whilst she was a very caring mother, the lady, like most Indian mothers, was protective of her son Saravanan who had bad habits. He had dropped out of school but taken on a job and faithfully went to work. He made his monthly contribution to the household knowing fully well his parents earned meagre sums and worked long hours.

Smoking was the youth's main problem. The only person he would listen to was his 16-year-old girlfriend, a fair and pretty secondary four student. He had been with her for almost three years and they loved one another dearly. We learnt that Saravanan was devoted to the girl and made it a point to visit her daily; calling her or receiving calls from her daily was a routine and a must for him at all cost.

If the girl failed to call him, he would make it a point to visit her no matter what time of day it was. Did his parents object to his relationship with the 16-year-old student? His parents had raised objections in the beginning but soon accepted his love for the girl.

On the strength of the favourable probation report and on the positive undertaking by his parents to supervise Saravanan, Judge Reddy decided to place him on a 12-month probation. Before we could breathe a sigh of relief, we were shocked to see Saravanan back in court on yet another case of petty theft.

Mr Reddy was upset but chose to give the youth another chance. He felt very strongly that Saravanan deserved another chance. Having heard his family circumstances and having studied Viven's report on the youth, Judge was of the opinion Saravanan ought not to be sent to reformative training centre, although a repeat offender.

Another period of probation was apt under the circumstances Mr Reddy felt. "This boy can change. He is constantly disturbed by his craving for his girlfriend but his association with the girl does not seem too detrimental," he said.

The date of mention came. Saravanan and his mother appeared in open court. Judge addressed both the youth and his mother, reprimanded Saravanan for his repeat offending and cautioned the mother that the court would not be lenient anymore should Saravanan re-offend.

Saravanan was placed on probation with the usual conditions attached. I had a lot of interpreting to do for Judge as well as Viven who was directed to give a pep talk to both mother and son. Deep down in our hearts we were satisfied a good job had been done.

Some weeks later, I was at work one afternoon when I received a call from Shamu, the volunteer counsellor from the Hindu Centre following up on Saravanan's case. She said,

"Saravanan committed suicide." It was unbelievable. Stunned by the news I immediately called Mr Reddy. Mr Reddy's comment was, "I least would have expected this to happen."

Justice Punch Coomaraswamy

It was a murder trial. In the dock was an accused person facing a capital charge. Hearing the case were two judges, the late Justice Punch Coomaraswamy being one of them. Giving evidence for the prosecution was a translator from the police. For capital cases, the accused is not offered bail and as such is remanded in the custody of the police. Under these circumstances the court would have granted the police permission for the said accused to be interrogated, and in the course of doing so, record statement(s) from the accused. If the accused speaks the English language, the police officers would proceed to record statement(s) directly from the accused person. If the accused is not conversant in English and needs the assistance of an interpreter, the police will arrange for such assistance from its pool of interpreters. Interpreters will then assist the investigating officers to record statements.

The witness (translator) on the stand was asked to explain her role in the recording of the statement(s) from the accused. As the charge preferred was one of murder, the translator had used the term "murder" when referring to the killing of the victim which was the essence of the charge. At this point Justice Punch intercepted to explain the use of the word "murder". He explained that a mere killing did not constitute murder. Judge then went on to explain "murder" and its different limbs as set out in the Penal Code. Judge continued to explain that the term "murder" with its fullest meaning would have included the concept of pre-meditation – a pre-planned criminal intent to cause the death of the victim. "Killing", the judge further explained, was the act of causing the victim's death and this need not have been pre-planned. From Justice Punch's clear explanation the witness realised there was a stark difference between causing a person's death and committing a "murder". The witness, an experienced and trained officer, was grateful to the judge for the clarity in the use of the two terms and the analogies the judge had drawn in his explanation.

I listened very attentively to the Justice's explanation. I appreciated the short but clear lesson. I had until then been under the impression that "killing" and "murder" were synonymous and that the two terms could be used interchangeably. I went to read more on the topic as I found it interesting. I shared the knowledge I had acquired in court in that day's session with my colleagues.

It was about ten years into my service during the time of this incident. Young and energetic, with the drive to gain as much knowledge as possible, I followed up on reading submissions prepared by lawyers representing clients in capital cases. I soon developed a keen interest in reading verdicts by judges in capital cases. This certainly led to a better understanding of judges' guidance to parties involved in such cases.

I took a very special liking to Justice Punch and made myself available for cases heard by him. In later years Justice Punch became more involved in community work, especially in the rebuilding of the Sri Muneeswaran Temple at Commonwealth Drive. The judge served as the temple's patron; during this period I served as the temple's honorary secretary for ten years. I had occasion to meet the judge in his private chambers in the course of the temple's building which involved both the judge and myself for some years.

District Judge Tan Puay Boon

In the late 1990s when I was posted to the Family Court at Paterson Road, I was most fortunate to have worked with District Judge Tan Puay Boon, now Judicial Commissioner. We were not familiar with one another in the new Paterson environment.

During a night mediation session working on a difficult maintenance issue, I observed and learnt how an impressive tone and concerned human touch can reach out to two warring spouses! For the first time in my career, I heard a judge address an interpreter as "my colleague". Mr Tan stands out amongst his contemporaries as a judicial officer of no comparison!

Examples of pleasant, caring judicial officers can make an endless list. Most judges are down-to-earth and respectful towards interpreters. It cannot be denied however that there is a handful of judicial officers who, after a few months in the courts, don't hesitate to raise their voice when addressing officers in the courts even when these officers have more than two decades of experience!

How have I been treated by fellow court administrators? It is no exaggeration that I have always been well regarded by colleagues I worked with. I believe 'respect begets respect'!

Respect your colleagues and fellow workers, irrespective of their age and inexperience and you shall receive respect and admiration at all times. Have I found friends amongst my working colleagues? Yes, amongst the scores of colleagues I have worked with, the late Lashman Singh, Zakaria Ismail, Daniel Ang and V Pandiyan stand out as admirable friends!

The decision to stop work is a difficult and painful one. What will you do after giving up something which has kept you so very occupied, many had asked me? Close friends have seriously cautioned me: Boredom will set in. That may lead to mental fatigue and emotional stress, I was told. I quite see their point. I don't deny it. Too much free time can harm one. But does that mean one has to work perpetually till death?

Retiring Judge Chao Hick Tin as he was honoured on his retirement by the JOs of the State Courts. Both Judge Chao and I completed fifty years in the Civil Service in September 2017.

Judges and Court Administrators since 1975

(Left to Right)
First row: Principal District Judge **Tan Puay Boon**, Deputy Presiding Judge **Jennifer Marie**, Mr **Errol Foenander**, Judicial Commissioner **See Kee Oon**, Mr **Michael Khoo SC**, Principal Director **Bala Reddy**, Principal Director **James Leong**
Second row: Mr **Lau Wing Yum**, Mr **Alfonso Ang**, Judicial Commissioner **Hoo Sheau Peng**, Mr **Francis Remedios**, District Judge **Low Wee Ping**, Mr **Toh Han Li**

(Left to Right)
First row: Mr **Yong Yung Kiong**, Mr **Lee Cheong Hoh**, Mr **Khoo Oon Soo**, Mr **Tan Lian Ker**, Mr **Ibrahim Burhan**, Dr **S Chandra Mohan**, Mr **Francis Tseng**
Second row: Mr **Roy Neighbour**, District Judge **Hamidah Ibrahim**, District Judge **Liew Thiam Leng**, Judicial Commissioner **Foo Tuat Yien**, Mr **Leslie Chew SC**, Mr **Sarjit Singh**, District Judge **Tan Peck Cheng**

(Left to Right)
First row: Mr **Ismail Bin Mat**, Mrs **Yeow-Mak Yuen Ling**, Ms **Noraini Binte Haji Omar**, Ms **Anne Mathew**, Mr **Glenfield De Souza**, Mr **Sivanandan Nadarajoo**, Ms **Lucy Goh**, Ms **Carmen Seah**, Mrs **Mok-Goh Kit Soon**, Ms **Irene Lee**, Ms **Rosalind Yap**, Ms **Jennie Phua**, Ms **Teresa Teow**
Second row: Mr **James Chuah**, Mr **Manickam s/o Pr Periasamy**, Mr **Mohd Abdullah B Rahim**, Mr **Jumahat Bin Ahmad**, Mr **Ajmer Singh s/o Sohan Singh**, Mr **Chew Chuee Seng**, Mr **Lee Chun Yip**, Mr **Yong Siew Kin**, Mr **Richard Lau Boon Teow**, Mr **Lashman Singh s/o Thaman Singh**, Mr **Mohamed Yusof Bin Mohamed Arshad**, Mr **Joseph John**, Ms **Patricia Png**, Mr **Kok Long Seng**, Mr **Ng Han Cheong**, Mr **Cheong Yuen Kwan**

PART 2

OPENING OF THE LEGAL YEAR

Every January, the Supreme Court observes a ceremony called the Opening of the Legal Year. At this annual ceremony, this following phrase is pronounced as the Chief Justice goes to the bench to make his ceremonial address:

"ALL MANNER OF PERSONS HAVING ANYTHING TO DO WITH THE SITTING OF THE COURT DRAW NEAR AND GIVE YOUR ATTENDANCE."

THE JURY TRIAL

1. More than fifty years ago, there was in place in the Singapore judicial system, a restricted jury trial to try capital offences. According to this system, capital offences were tried by a single High Court Judge, assisted by a panel of twelve (12) laypersons.
2. The judge decided on the law pertaining to the charge the accused was facing. The jury decided on the facts borne out by the evidence in the trial.
3. In 1958, the jury system was introduced into the then Federation of Malaya, for all capital offences only. Jury trials for all offences continued in the legal system until 1976 when it was restricted to capital offences only.
4. In 1960, Singapore also restricted jury trial to capital offences and abolished the system altogether in 1970.
5. This is produced from *The Malayan Law Report* for interesting reading:

The Prime Minister, Mr Lee Kuan Yew, delivered the keynote speech during the second reading, stressing the premium the jury system placed on a lawyer's *"skill and agility", and the fact that trial by jury did not mean trial by one's peers but trial by the English-educated. He did, however, admit that the jury trial as "a foreign implantation" worked "reasonably well", but required a "very high degree of skill from the Bar and the Bench" and witnesses who were in fact willing to come forward. Justice was being thwarted on "pure technicalities" and reference was made to the Green Bus murder case*. Judges could make up their minds on facts as well as the jurymen could and the amendment would bring our system into line with Malaya's.*

---

* *Where the conviction was quashed on appeal owing to a misdirection by the trial judge: Ong Ah Too v. R., (1955) 21 M.L.J. 247.*

JUDICIAL COMMITTEE OF THE PRIVY COUNCIL

The Judicial Committee consists of senior judges appointed as Privy Counsellors: predominantly Justices of the Supreme Court of the United Kingdom and senior judges from the Commonwealth.

It is often referred to as the Privy Council, as in most cases appeals are nominally made to 'Her Majesty in Council' (i.e. the British monarch as formally advised by her Privy Counsellors), who then refer the case to the Judicial Committee for 'advice.' The panel of judges (typically five in number) hearing a particular case is known as 'the Board'. The 'report' of the Board is always accepted by the Queen in Council as judgment.

Initially, all Commonwealth realms and their territories maintained a right of appeal to the Privy Council. Many of those Commonwealth countries that became republics, or which had indigenous monarchies, preserved the Judicial Committee's jurisdiction by agreement with the United Kingdom.

However, retention of a right of appeal to a court located overseas, made up mostly of British judges who may be out of tune with local values, has often come to be seen as incompatible with notions of an independent nation's sovereign status, and so a number of Commonwealth members have ended the right of appeal from their jurisdiction. The

Balfour Declaration of 1926, while not considered to be *lex scripta*, severely limited the conditions under which the Judicial Committee might hear cases.

Malaysia abolished appeals to the Privy Council in criminal and constitutional matters in 1978, and in civil matters in 1985.

Singapore abolished Privy Council appeals in all cases save those involving the death penalty, or in civil cases where the parties had agreed to such a right of appeal, in 1989. The abolition followed a decision of the Privy Council the previous year that criticised the "grievous injustice" suffered by the opposition politician J B Jeyaretnam at the hands of the Government of Singapore. The remaining rights of appeal were abolished in 1994.

PLEA OF CLEMENCY

Since Singapore's independence, seven clemencies have been granted. Two were granted in the term of President Benjamin Sheares, one under President Devan Nair, three under President Wee Kim Wee, and one under President Ong Teng Cheong.

When an accused in a capital case is convicted, he is at liberty to appeal against the judge's decision in the Court of Criminal Appeal. Such appeals are heard before three judges in the Court of Appeal. Counsel for the appellant will submit to the three judges' arguments against the trial judge's findings for the conviction.

Representing the State, the Deputy Public Prosecutor will advance rebuttal arguments supporting the trial judge's decision. The hearing in this instance will centre around submissions made by defence counsel and the prosecuting officer. At the end of the submissions, the trial judges would deliver their verdict, either allowing or dismissing the appeal. There are instances where the judges would postpone verdict in order to deliberate on arguments put forward for and against the appellant.

If the Court of Appeal dismisses the appeal, the accused would face the death penalty. At this juncture, the appellant is open to putting up a Plea of Clemency. This is in the form of a petition to the President of the Republic. The Constitution grants the President powers to make a decision on the appeal.

This therefore serves as a last opportunity for the appellant to save himself from the gallows.

The papers to be sent to the President are prepared by the appellant's counsel who probably would have represented him (the appellant) at the initial hearing before a single judge and again before the three judges who constitute the Court of Appeal. Plea of Clemency or Presidential Pardon is power invested with the President of the Republic to show an appellant leniency. The President, however, discharges this duty under the Constitution, in consultation with the Cabinet's advice.

In showing leniency, the President first receives a petition for clemency. Such petition is prepared by the lawyer representing the appellant convicted of a crime or crimes. The offender's sentence could be reduced or the offender totally relieved of his sentence.

In granting the offender convicted of an offence, the President is also empowered to grant a pardon to an accomplice also convicted by the same court. Often petition for clemency is sought by persons sentenced to death usually for capital cases. On presenting this petition before the President, the convict would have exhausted all avenues of appeal and this will serve as a last resort for the convict.

The judges who had tried the accused and convicted him or her will be approached to present reports on the case. Such report(s) are then forwarded to the Attorney-General's (AG) Chambers for their opinions. The AG then forwards this to the Cabinet, which advises the President whether to grant the offender the clemency sought.

Readers may have heard of the term "President's pleasure". Very simply explained this term means an offender is detained indefinitely until such time he or she is found fit for release.

When the offender is detained in custody, his conduct will be closely monitored by prison authorities. His case is periodically reviewed so as to determine when the offender should be released.

Some cases where a plea of clemency was made

A teenager who was an accomplice to Anthony Ler, and had plotted the murder of Anthony Ler's wife, was released on 2 November 2018 when the President Halimah Yacob granted the said petitioner's plea of clemency. The release of the teenager, now 32 years old came about after he had served 17 years behind bars.

His release was subject to conditions such as curfew hours and electronic monitoring. There is a gag order on his identity because of his age when he committed the crime. The teenager was 15 years old when he stabbed the victim multiple times in May 2001. The Court had found him guilty of murder in December 2002.

Parents of Malaysian Michael Garing had sent a clemency plea for their son's life to the Republic's President. Michael, convicted of murder by the Singapore High Court was scheduled for execution on Friday 22 March 2019 in Singapore.

Michael and another Sarawakian, Tony Imba, were part of a gang that went on a robbery sphere, severely injuring three victims and killing a fourth man in 2010.

President Halimah Yacob (in consultation with the cabinet) rejected the plea of clemency by Michael Garing. Michael's plea had been supported by Malaysia's Prime Minister, Mahathir Mohamed. Michael was executed as scheduled.

REFERENCES FOR THE CASES MENTIONED

1. Four men accused of raping nurses, *The Strait Times*, 9 January 1969, Page 9
2. *Mohamed Kunjo v Public Prosecutor* [1977–1978] SLR(R) 211
3. *Public Prosecutor v Visuvanathan* [1978] 1 MLJ 159
4. *N Govindasamy v Public Prosecutor* [1976] 2 MLJ 49
5. *Public Prosecutor v Selvraj Subramanian* [1984–1985] SLR 488
6. *Public Prosecutor v Ramasamy A/L Sebastian* [1990] 2 SLR(R) 197
7. *Public Prosecutor v Nadunjalian s/o Rajoo* [1993] SGHC 32, [1993] 2 SLR(R) 316
8. *Sinniah Pillay v Public Prosecutor* [1991] 2 SLR(R) 704
9. Woman jailed for life for throwing boy to his death, *The Strait Times*, 9 October 1993, Page 26
10. *Public Prosecutor v Victor Rajoo s/o A Pitchay Muthu* [1995] SGHC 157
11. Public Prosecutor v Nadasan Chandra Secharan [1996] SGHC 228, [1997] 1 SLR(R) 118
12. *Public Prosecutor v Perumal Naidu Surendra Sean Clinton & others* [2004] SGDC 129
13. *Public Prosecutor v G Krishnasamy Naidu* [2006] SGHC 44
14. *Public Prosecutor v Rajendran Mohan* [2015] SGDC 54

"A person is either a born interpreter, or is not ... the job is extremely difficult. It is not a mechanical one. It is a job where you need tremendous speed and clarity of thought and great strength of mind ...."

AT Pilley
Renowned linguist, conference interpreter,
and principal of the Linguists' Club, London.